Advance Praise for *Working With Humans*

In a world in which machines and tools seem to be ruling us and forcing us to accommodate their capacities, Laura Crandall reminds us of the proper dignity of being human. Her voice is a clarion call of hope, an invitation to recover our full humanity by transforming the way we talk to one another.

Frank Barrett, PhD
Professor, Department of Organizational Behavior,
Weatherhead School of Management
Author of *Yes to the Mess*

If you want to learn how to make those "sticky situations at work unstick", read this book! Laura's insightful, practical, and laugh-out-loud funny guidance is the companion guide we all need as we navigate relationships at work. This is not just a 'how to' guide. Laura's wisdom calls on us to see and to live our inherent potential as we navigate the realities of our shared humanity at work.

Julie Jungalwala
President, Academic Leadership Group
Author of *The Human Side of Changing Education*

This book is a highly practical collection of tools for improving communication in organizations based on decades of work. It is also laugh-out-loud funny, accessible, and most importantly, hopeful.

Timothy O'Brien, EdD
Lecturer in Public Policy, Harvard Kennedy School

Laura Crandall has decades of experience leading and consulting to management teams of every ilk. Over that time, she noticed that there were several basic skills missing from most managers' toolboxes. In this well-written and fun book she identifies those missing tools and offers them in a practical framework that makes them easy to practice and apply. Since we all work with humans it's important to humanize our workplaces and this book shows you how.

Richard Schwartz, PhD
Developer of the Internal Family Systems Model
Author of *No Bad Parts*

I have worked with Laura for more than a decade and she has shaped the way I interact with my team and guided me in developing our company culture. Whether you are a team member or a leader, I can confidently say that this book is a game-changer. It's also fun and engaging. You won't be sorry you bought it.

Jessica Andreola Parker
CEO, Kusshi

Informed by Crandall's expertise in cognitive neuroscience and organizational behavior along with anecdotes from her varied work experience from fish canning to massage therapy to management consulting, this lively, witty book offers a refreshing take on the communication "tools we need but rarely talk about." Her Character Compass, Four Things to Do Forever, and Key Behaviors (including "Don't Be a Jackass"), plus the book's useful activities, can relieve our "management-model whiplash," helping us "act for, not from, our emotions" as we emerge from pandemic-era isolation and once again work with humans in the workplace.

Catherine Johnston
Professor, Clark College - ESL

WORKING WITH HUMANS

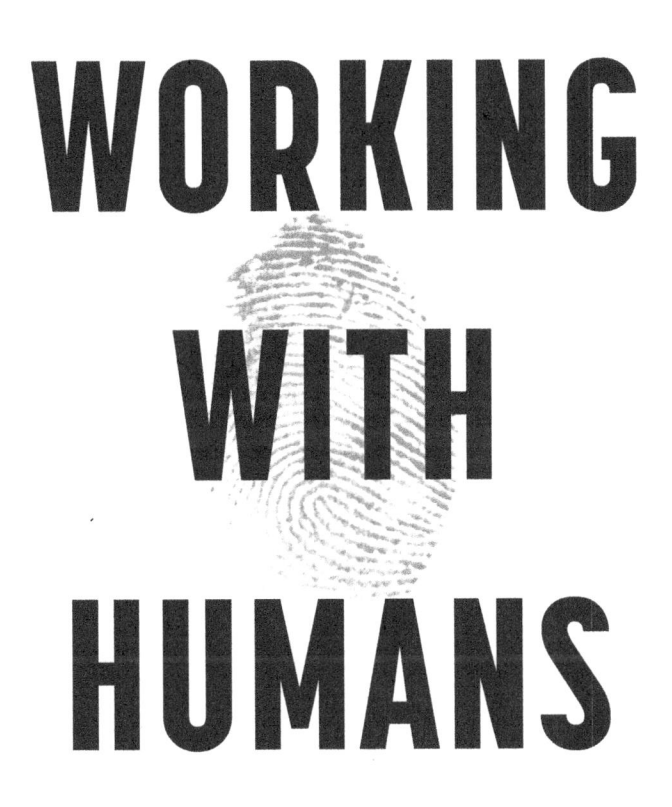

Tools You Didn't Know You Needed for
Conversations You Never Expected to Have

LAURA CRANDALL

BANQUET
PUBLISHING

WORKING WITH HUMANS

TOOLS YOU DIDN'T KNOW YOU NEEDED FOR CONVERSATIONS YOU NEVER EXPECTED TO HAVE

BY **LAURA CRANDALL**

YOU NEED **CURIOSITY** TO BEGIN

NEEDED FOR EVERYTHING ELSE

CHARACTER COMPASS

the hill you don't need to die on

forest of remedies

SOLITARY WORK THAT BEARS FRUIT WHEN SHARED WITH OTHERS

YOU ARE IN SOME SORT OF SITUATION

abyss of cynicism

political quagmire

orchard of fruitful effort

unicorn in a hay stack

USE & FINE TUNE YOUR CHARACTER COMPASS

YOU NEED TOOLS, LEARNING, AND PRACTICE

YOUR ESSENTIAL TOOLS

CHARACTER COMPASS

KEY BEHAVIORS / COMMUNICATION / CONTEXT

SHOW ME THE WAY

PAUSE. BREATHE. YOU ARE GOING TO MAKE IT THROUGH.

YOU ARE HERE

ADD THESE TOOLS TO ELIMINATE ANNOYING MISCOMMUNICATION AND POOR BEHAVIOR

FEELING STUCK? DON'T GET FURIOUS. GET CURIOUS.

COMPASS IS USED FROM HERE ON OUT

your **CHARACTER** = **VALUES ENACTED** over **TIME**

YOU ARE RESPONSIBLE FOR YOUR OWN CHARACTER & BEHAVIOR

PREPARE FOR THE UNEXPECTED

moral quicksand

ego cliff

THINGS MAY BE CALM; YOU'RE LOOKING TO MEANDER AND GET SOME SKILLS.

OR MAYBE THINGS ARE IN CRISIS MODE...

OR SOMEWHERE IN BETWEEN

ASSESS your **TASK OR SITUATION**

WHAT ARE YOUR EXPECTATIONS & HOPES REGARDING WORK?

** WE ASSUME WE KNOW WHAT THIS IS. BUT WE DON'T OFTEN CHECK TO SEE IF WE ARE CORRECT

A | B | C | D

COMMUNICATION MUST HAVES:

requires constant calibration

CORE QUESTIONS:
- WHY
- WHAT
- HOW
- IF

waterfall of hope

4 THINGS TO DO FOREVER

1. COMMUNICATE CLEARLY
2. SET EXPECTATIONS
3. GET COMMITMENT
4. FOLLOW THROUGH

These allow you to be clear

Remember personal reflection

PRACTICE WITH A PAL

EXPECTATIONS INVENTORY

too much of any of these is bad. needs balance to work

soft rocks drink water

navigate core questions

MAGIC ANSWER DOWNLOAD

disappointing and satisfying situations

brighter horizons

hills of collaboration

WE EXPECT THESE BEHAVIORS — DON'T FORGET TO TALK ABOUT AND SHARE THEM.

EXPECTATIONS WORK BEST WHEN DISCUSSED DIRECTLY.

Personal & cultural evolution

KEY BEHAVIORS
The behaviors with which you work, communicate & manage

① MANNERS & KINDNESS
② BE OF HELP
③ PRIDE IN YOUR WORK
④ DON'T BE A JACKASS

Behaviors are needed to make other tools work best

These influence every choice & action and are informed by your character

coast of hard truths

NEW DEPTHS

MAP BY STEF KOEHLER © 2023

Copyright © 2023 by Laura Crandall

All rights reserved. No part of this publication may be reproduced, stored in a retrieval system, or transmitted in any form or by any means, without prior permission in writing from the publisher. This includes use in any manner for purposes of training artificial intelligence technologies to generate text, including without limitation, technologies that are capable of generating works in the same style or genre as this publication.

Library of Congress Control Number: 2023940778

Paperback ISBN: 979-8-9882254-1-6
E-book ISBN: 979-8-9882254-0-9

Also available in audiobook.

Cover and text design by Alex Hennig
Map illustration by Stef Koehler
Interior illustrations by Molly Russell

Banquet Publishing

Belmont, MA, USA
banquetpublishing.com

Privacy and Names

I have changed the names of people in the stories and examples within this book. Exceptions are noted.

*For Karen, my mom.
Learning to be a friend is a
generous and courageous endeavor.
Thank you for sharing your
expertise and rich friendship with me.*

*For Jim, my dad.
Because in math and in life,
if you don't understand the story,
you'll never understand the problem.
Thank you for the delight of curiosity.*

Contents

Introduction	**1**
How to Use This Book	**11**
Orientation	**13**
Learning About and Using Your Tools	
Your Character Compass	**27**
Essential Tool #1: Your Character Compass	27
Using and Fine-Tuning Your Character Compass	34
Unexpected Conversations	46
Practice With a Pal	48
What's in It for YOU	51
The Communication Must-Haves	**55**
Essential Tool #2:	
The Communication Must-Haves	55
Core Questions — Curiosity Starts Here	59
Four Things to Do Forever — Let's Get Clear	68
Unexpected Conversations	89
Practice With a Pal	91
What's in It for YOU	93
The Key Behaviors	**99**
Essential Tool #3: The Key Behaviors	100
The Key Behaviors	101
Unexpected Conversations	130
Practice With a Pal	132
What's in It for YOU	135
Conclusion	**141**

Next Steps	**143**
Navigating Your Way	**144**
Acknowledgments	**147**
References	**149**
Additional Resources	**152**
About the Author	**154**

WORKING WITH HUMANS

TOOLS YOU DIDN'T KNOW YOU NEEDED FOR CONVERSATIONS YOU NEVER EXPECTED TO HAVE

BY LAURA CRANDALL

the hill you don't need to die on

forest of remedies

SOLITARY WORK THAT BEARS FRUIT WHEN SHARED WITH OTHERS

YOU ARE IN SOME SORT OF SITU...

orchard of fruitful effort

YOU NEED TOOLS, LEARNING, AND PRACTICE

SHOW ME THE WAY

PAUSE. BREATHE. YOU ARE GOING TO MAKE IT THROUGH.

ADD THESE TOOLS TO ELIMINATE ANNOYING MISCOMMUNICATION AND POOR BEHAVIOR

FEELING STUCK? DON'T GET FURIOUS. GET CURIOUS.

PREPARE FOR THE UNEXPECTED

moral quicksand

THINGS MAY BE CALM; YOU'RE LOOKING TO MEANDER AND GET SOME SKILLS.

OR MAYBE THINGS ARE IN CRISIS MODE...

OR SOMEWHERE IN BETWEEN

ASSESS *your* TASK OR SITUATION**

WHAT ARE YOUR EXPECTATIONS & HOPES REGARDING WORK?

**WE ASS... KNOW WHAT BUT WE DON... CHECK TO SEE ARE CORR...

Introduction

Now is a great time to become good at working with humans.

It is likely that you're reading this book because you are facing a situation that involves both *humans* and *work*. Maybe you want to be able to manage yourself well so you can work anywhere with minimal miscommunication and strife. Maybe you are new to a management role and want a few pointers on how to connect with your team. Maybe you have been in a leadership role for a while and just don't understand why employees cannot commit to deadlines. Maybe you are so tired of the people you work with and their unending cluelessness that you are considering selling everything you own and moving to the Yukon just to get away from them. Whatever the reason, you are not alone. We're all dealing with situations at work that can be concerning, confusing, or crazy-making. At the root of each one is a communication problem: the problem of not having and using the core tools we need to communicate well with each other.

You may be thinking, "What? How can that be true? This is the Information Age. We communicate all day long. We have every app, device, and method there is. How can tools be the problem?" You're right, we communicate all day long and have a zillion ways to do it. Access isn't the issue. Our approach to our interactions and our awareness of *how* we communicate is. The general method most workplaces use to handle daily problems is to apply a formulaic process: Tell people to follow instructions, be directive, and demand their attention and compliance—mission accomplished. That approach never works for long. What's missing are the foundational tools and core qualities that make interpersonal communication *work* in our workplaces. This book helps you acquire and understand those tools, then build confidence in using them well.

∞

Clients ask me lots of questions at my management and communication consultancy, Slate Communication. Most of them are variations of:

1. Why are people so annoying to work with?
2. Why aren't the things I'm doing to manage people working in the ways I think they should?

The short answers are:

1. Because people just *are* annoying—and we're also pretty wonderful.
2. Because we neglect learning and practicing the essential communication tools that are vital to working well with other humans.

The more complete answer to these questions has two important parts. The first part is that we struggle with the people we work with because, despite all our shared intelligence, aptitude, and skill, we're mostly making it up as we go along. We rely on a blend of luck, interpersonal momentum, and prayers to the gods of workplace politics that we will be able to get along with our colleagues. These things help to a point, but 99% of issues at work are anchored in miscommunication and unmet expectations.[1] *Our problems exist because we don't know how to talk with each other.* We aren't taught to communicate well, yet we assume we're competent ... as if by magic.

The second part is more complex and more painful. On top of being unskilled in how we communicate, there is an underlying and unexpected basis for our workplace troubles: being seen as a valued human being often feels impossible. That's because, in the United States, recognizing

---

1 This is probably an underestimate, but I wanted to leave room for things like quicksand, lightning bolts, and spontaneous combustion.

and honoring the annoyances, complexities, and glorious beauty of being human goes against how work *itself* was initially designed to operate.

If we want to get better at working together as humans, we must address the uncomfortable truth that the importance of human dignity has never been a focal point in the U.S. industrial system. While people have always been able to find meaning and satisfaction from their labor (having pride in one's work is an important topic in this book), those have been personal by-products of a system that prioritizes productivity over the humans who create it. The centuries-old paradigm that has shaped how businesses operate and become profitable was problematic at its inception: profits, growth, and expansion were possible because white people in positions of colonial power enslaved Black and Brown people to produce goods made from land stolen from Indigenous people. That dominant framework, and the long-term consequences of its efficacy in creating profit, is antithetical to valuing the people who *do* the work.

That said, productivity sustained through exploitation of workers is not the whole story—far from it. Businesses and organizations of all types work hard to operate in ways that challenge the status quo and how companies are "supposed to" function.[2] They make the world of work better in the process. *You* are making it better simply by being curious and reading this book—and you are in good company. So many people are participating in redesigning the way we work. This requires deliberate effort and care.

But our past and our present are full of businesses and systems that have become comfortable—and highly successful—within a structure that says human labor is there to be used in indiscriminate ways.[3] Much of the frustration and malaise you may feel about the command-and-con-

---

2 Those organizations sincerely dedicated to the sustainability model of a triple bottom line (people, planet, and profit) are excellent examples of efforts to change the world of work. Many workplaces are reimagining what a "full-time" workweek looks like, and companies that actively align their environmental and social footprint with their espoused values are shaping our understanding of how business can benefit the world.

3 When bosses say, "Our people are our greatest asset," it's a strange compliment that objectifies human beings. It feels awkwardly creepy. I feel the same about the term *Human Resources*. Both make me think of the 1999 classic film *The Matrix* and its towering pods of human batteries. The older term *Personnel* has a friendlier ring to my ear.

trol, production-focused habits of your workplace makes sense because the original blueprint for such productivity—volume of goods and speed of output are more important than your human life—feels really yucky. Yet this cultural disposition is so intertwined with the economy and buried in our collective psyche that it is nearly impossible to separate the harmful aspects of productivity from its helpful capacity for beneficence and contribution in the world around us. Productivity without regard for people and place is damaging, but we have become hypnotized by the fact that it's an easy way to get stuff done. And that makes it all too easy to discount the communication skills I'm sharing with you in this book.

Conversations about feeling overwhelmed and managing the inevitability of burnout are now included as part of college curricula to brace students for working life. Aspirations of work-life balance often feel laughably out of reach. What must we do when this giant flaw in our system can no longer be overlooked? We must address the fact that the human aspect—the *humanity*—of the labor required to be profitable and expansive was subjugated and discounted from the beginning. **We, the humans involved, have to infuse humanity into the design.**

You are in an oddly perfect circumstance to address this problem and transform the way you work—and how others around you work, too. By rediscovering and reclaiming simple tools of personal behavior, you can reconnect your humanity to your labor—one interaction and one conversation at a time. When you learn to talk about what drives your choices, to clarify expectations with another human, and thus create a shared trust in respectful workplace behaviors, you can decrease the annoyance level and increase the humanity in your workplace. Yes, *you* can do all that. Now is the perfect time to imagine how you want your work life to feel and help make it happen. This may sound idealistic. It's also true.

Nice to Meet You

If we met at a networking event or started chatting in line at a coffee shop[4] and you asked me what I do for work, I would probably respond by asking you, "Do you work with other people? Do you have a boss or colleagues?"

You'd likely say, "Yes, I do."

"What do you like most about working with them?"

Your answer would probably be a little vague and generally polite.

I'd ask you, "What frustrates you about working with them? What situations make you roll your eyes?"

Your energy would shift and your responses would become more specific and animated: you've got an example from today. Or three. What you'd say next is something I've heard, in some form, a thousand times. That's not to say your complaint isn't unique to your experience—it is. It's because we all have things that irritate us about our coworkers. Our bosses. Our direct reports. Our clients. Our vendors.

After you tell me what bugs you, I'd gently point out where in your story it sounds like expectations weren't specific, where unnecessary confusion sprang up because your team was not communicating clearly, where there were faulty assumptions about what each person was doing and why. I'd say it's likely that no one has explained the context of your work or its importance for the future of your organization. Communication and interactions are difficult because everyone is coming at them from a different angle.

"Exactly!" you'd shout, glad to be understood.

That's how I'd tell you what I do. "I help you learn the tools that make those sticky situations unstick. Those frustrations that get in the way of good strategy, effective use of talent and expertise, and the joy of a job well done—I teach you how to prevent them. I help make working with humans easier."

---

4   Yes, I am one of those people who likes to chat in line. I also smile and talk with people in elevators. Turns out, it's even good for you. See Susan Pinker's 2017 TED Talk and her 2015 book, *The Village Effect*.

INTRODUCTION   5

I founded my management consulting firm in 2009. I spent the fifteen years before that managing teams and leading organizations. The tools in this book are the result of over thirty years' experience working in and consulting with industries that include manufacturing, hospitality, journalism, and academia. I've tested the tools you are about to learn in organizations of all shapes, sizes, and dispositions: privately held software companies, philanthropic divisions of publicly traded tech giants, small interior design firms, award-winning distilleries, alternative energy companies, small colleges, and Ivy League universities. Every single one of them needed the tools in this book, and none of them—no matter how successful or famous—knew the importance of learning to use them. That missing knowledge caused innumerable mistakes and plenty of unnecessary suffering.

How was it, you may ask, that I managed to identify these vital yet weirdly absent communication tools in so many different organizations? It was a combination of being a workplace superfan,[5] having a deep commitment to helping people create work and workplaces that feel meaningful, earning my master's degree from Harvard Graduate School of Education (where I studied cognitive neuroscience and organizational behavior), being a very curious nerd, and paying close attention to the patterns of what didn't work when working with humans over my long and varied work life. I have been lucky to have had an excellent career working with great people in a variety of industries and situations. I've experienced the good, the bad, and the weird in all of them.

How good, bad, or weird?

I have made a living sliming fish in an Alaskan cannery. That job included being elbow-deep in fish guts in cold, wet, sometimes dangerous conditions, and working sixteen-hour days, seven days a week. I was injured more than once.

---

5   I'm also a straight, cis, Gen-X, white woman. My experience of work is through those lenses—a perspective I am constantly broadening, and one I endeavor to use for good and not for ill.

I have worked in a children's psychiatric hospital with kids who endured things that would boil your blood and break your heart. I have been a prep cook and made coleslaw and egg salad until I reeked of cabbage and sulfur. I've scrubbed toilets and done massive amounts of laundry. I have worked in college admissions. I've investigated discrimination and harassment claims. I've worked as a massage therapist and dealt with people who believed that they could be profoundly rude because of their net worth. I have shoveled shit, both literally and figuratively, in many industries for over three decades.

In all that time, I only disliked the work I was doing once: at the snack counter of a swim club when I was in high school. The job was boring, and not even free access to the pool made it worthwhile. I have, however, disliked a few workplaces. The worst was when I got a job that I needed badly, but the company's bleak and hyperefficient disposition drained the humor and interest out of employees the moment they walked in the door each day. No one talked to one another, and the place was ominously silent. It was like working in a morgue—but in a bad way.

That experience was a perfect example of a company with a problematic design, poor communication skills, lots of unspoken expectations, and no interest in engaging the talents, capacities, and energy of the people who made the company run.

Circumstances like that one, and many others, led to my commitment to helping people have better experiences at work. This book seeks to remedy these very common problems and address the behavioral assumptions and structural flaws in how our organizations operate. The tools you're about to learn can solve the question of why people are so annoying at work. These tools will give you a way to discuss the cultural norms that we all assume everyone knows as well as the things you suspect *you* should know but are afraid to ask. They provide a way to be generous with your coworkers, especially in the many awkward, frustrating, and surprising situations that arise at work.

The paradigm of productivity at the expense of humanity can feel too huge to fix. But you can be part of the solution to that big problem when you learn one powerful truth: *your daily choices and actions make your work culture.*

When you know how to work with other humans using specific, essential, practical tools, you make a real difference in the effectiveness and quality of your professional relationships and interactions—and you change the world for the better.

Blissfully Boring

The tools that follow are the ones I've identified over thirty-plus years as the tools we all need to have and use but rarely talk about. They are also the things that, when absent, cause the most distress and disappointment at work. I'll tell you the glaring truth now: they are not sexy—at all. They are boring, occasionally difficult, and may feel pretty awkward as you get started.

But the stuff organizations have been doing—the sexy management models that leaders learn at weekend retreats and then impose on staff until something new and improved comes along—aren't working that well.[6] Plus, management-model whiplash is exhausting.[7] So let's try something fundamental, simple, and boring instead. I think you'll like that it makes working with humans easier.

You can apply the tools in this book to whatever you're already doing at work. Whether you're working on a mission statement, planning a team outing to an escape room, onboarding a new employee, or just trying to get Greg from Accounting to be on time for meetings, you don't have to change operational strategies or learn a new management methodology. Just add these tools and keep doing what you're doing.[8]

---

6 If your organization is all about Agile, Blue Ocean, 7-S, Nudge Theory, or is still rocking Six-Sigma, these tools help make those models more beneficial to the people operating within them.

7 This is my unofficial term for the experience of people in workplaces everywhere when their boss goes to a seminar and returns ready to impose the shiny new model of management on their unsuspecting colleagues ... which lasts until the next seminar they attend to figure out why the last model isn't working.

8 There is one exception to this, but you'll learn about it in the chapter on The Key Behaviors: if you're being a jackass, please stop.

> **Please note: The essential and wildly under-discussed tools herein are not a management model. That's not their purpose. Their purpose is to help make your current model work better. Think of them like a laundry booster for the workplace: when you add a generous scoop of these essential skills to what you're already doing, you eliminate the unappealing stains and odors of miscommunication and poor behavior.**

This book gives you the foundational tools and core elements of management and communication, broken down, so you can actually use them now to gain confidence in yourself and the people you work with. These are vital to every person's success because they are the foundations for responsible management of yourself, your choices, and the quality of your interactions—regardless of whether you supervise others. The result? Less annoyance, better connections, increased confidence, and an improvement to the design flaw in a system that neglects the humanity in our work. Sound good? Let's start Working With Humans.

How to Use This Book

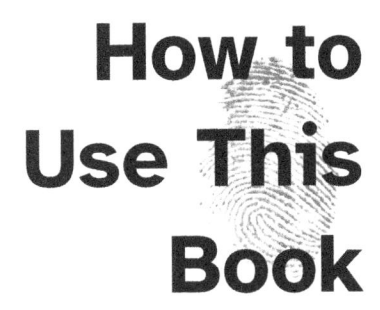

Making the Most of *Working With Humans*:

1. Skim through the book. Look for worksheets, practice conversations, lists, and sidebars to get a feel for things.
2. Note what you are drawn to. Are there certain topics that make you think, "YES! This is the problem we have at work!" Write those down. If you manage other humans and you find your list is only about *their* work, be sure and add topics that apply to *you*, too (you have to work with yourself every day). As you practice with the tools, try them out on the actual problems you face at work. Identify the tasks that are easy and the ones that need extra effort.
3. Note the points that make you irritated or concerned. If something makes you think, "Well, that's total crap," write it down. Revisit this list and evaluate it as you experiment with the tools. Perhaps your perspective will shift as you practice.
4. I recommend starting at the beginning and working your way through each section, but if there is something else that you want to start with, go for it. Just make sure you go through all the exercises and chapters at some point—each piece supports the others and builds on what came before. Then you'll have a better understanding of the ideas and tools.

5. Once you've read the book and worked through the exercises, share what you've learned with a trusted friend. Then use the book with your team and your department. The humanity you bring into each conversation will make working with humans better every day.
6. If you manage others, you may find yourself thinking only as a manager who is trying to improve things and get others to change. I understand that habit, but *please read this book primarily as a human who works with humans*. If you use these tools only as a way to "fix" other people without first applying them to yourself, your efforts won't go very far. Every human is responsible for managing their own behaviors and attitudes *first*—that's true whether you're a CEO or about to start your first job. We all need the same essential tools to communicate well.

Orientation

Essential Tools

The day I started to understand that these were the essential tools every human needs at work, it was a beautiful April morning in Cambridge, Massachusetts. The flowering trees were full of the bright pinks and electric greens so welcome after the cold, gray winter.

I was schlepping a box of flipchart paper and my satchel of Sharpies, Post-its, and stickers into an ivy-covered building at Harvard University. My mission for the day was to teach a team of researchers and educators how to create an easier, better-connected service experience for their patrons.

The day was so much fun. What I taught landed well, and the room filled with a palpable feeling of relief that the challenges these educators were facing had a solution. I remember thinking, "Pay attention to what you did today. It's important."

Two days later, I was in Burlington, Vermont—flip charts, Sharpies, and Post-its in hand—to work with a group of hospitality professionals about to open a beautiful and unique hotel. My mission was to teach them how to communicate effectively with their guests and each other while providing a welcoming and community-focused experience for everyone. I was there to teach service professionals how to think like educators.

The sessions went well and what I shared prompted engaged conversations and clear plans to start using their new knowledge. It was thrilling to watch managers and line staff become confident in how they could share the values behind their brand and hospitality. Again, I said to myself, "Remember this; it's important."

I still remember it, over a decade later. What made that week so important for me and shaped my work, and the essential tools in this book, was the realization that though the organizations were wildly different, what I taught both groups was the same.[9]

University educators and hotel staff don't often think of themselves as needing the same skills to be successful, but they do. And so do you. working with humans and putting humanity into our workplaces is needed everywhere and is no small task, but it needs to be done if we want to have more satisfying and fewer annoying experiences at work. It doesn't matter what your industry is. These are the tools that you need in order to eliminate frustration and increase clarity, satisfaction, and joy.

Everything that makes working with humans more effective revolves around three Essential Tools. They are like a decoder ring, magic wand, and your most comfortable pair of shoes all rolled into one: they will help you understand your colleagues, transform interactions for the better, and give you a confident spring in your step. The Essential Tools will keep you grounded, focused, and calm as you work with humans. They are:

1. **Your Character Compass**
2. **The Communication Must-Haves**
3. **The Key Behaviors**

---

9 The examples I share are taken from working with my clients. My perspective is the one that I have. My hope is that—whatever work you're doing and whoever you are—these examples can be of use to you.

Everything comes back to these three tools. They intertwine and build off each other. In any activity—cooking, dancing, playing basketball, surfing, doing math, writing, playing guitar, welding—there are foundational principles that everyone needs to do well. The same is true for working with humans.

Character, communication, and key behaviors are principles and skills we want to rely on but don't learn to use well at work.[10] That makes working with each other far harder than it needs to be. Imagine how difficult it would be to surf if you didn't know how to swim. What would happen if you wanted to cook but didn't know that heat was an important aspect of making food both safe and delicious? What if you were a scientist who needed to understand mathematics to check your experiments, but you never had a solid grip on how to multiply and divide? In any of those scenarios, the experience would be agonizing and more than a little perilous.

By being curious about our character, communication, and behavior, we gain insight into working well with other people. The most direct way

---

10 Part of the aversion to discussing these topics at work may have to do with the idea that these three areas tap into things that religions have had locked for a few millennia: hearts, words, and deeds. Just as this book is not a management model, it absolutely is not a discourse on religion.

to learn these skills is to notice the status of the Essential Tools in yourself. How frequently do you think about these? How comfortable do you feel talking about them?

1. **Character** is about being aligned with the qualities that make up your values. When you are true to your character, you have calm, openhearted confidence in who you are as a human being.
   - Understanding your character and its attributes can help build emotional maturity and skill in daily life. How you manage emotional choices can be regulated and supported by character.
   - Conscience and character are connected. Conscience is the generous (not judgmental) internal voice that encourages you to make choices that are aligned with your character—it's rooting for you.

2. **Communication** is about how you express yourself to yourself and to others.
   - You communicate with people in so many ways, and verbal language is just one element.
   - Body language and emotional expression are also ways to communicate with others. When all modes of communication—language, posture, attitudes—match and signify the same things, your effectiveness as a communicator improves.

3. **Behavior** is about the things that you do and the choices you make.
   - Actions are how we communicate character.
   - Behavioral expectations need to be shared—they are part of what makes working with humans *work*. If you don't know what others expect and they don't know what you expect, workplaces can become confusing pretty fast.

You may notice that *thoughts* are not mentioned in that list. Thoughts are something we use all the time to make sense of things, so think of them as a thread that ties character, communication, and behaviors together.[11] Thoughts help you reflect and evaluate. For our purposes here—regain-

---

[11] Feelings are a connecting thread, too. We'll talk about them in your First Assignment.

ing our humanity as we work with humans—we're going to be *thinking* about all three of these areas all the time. Then we're going to practice, practice, practice.

Preparing for the Unexpected

The Unexpected Conversations

If you work with other people, one thing is certain: you're going to have conversations you never expected to have. Lots of them. An unexpected conversation can be one that someone brings to you or that you bring to them. It doesn't have to be negative, but it is surprising nonetheless.

An unexpected conversation may be about a topic that feels so basic you feel stunned to mention it:

- "Yes, personal hygiene is an important social construct that needs to be followed."
- "No, racist and sexist comments are never okay, even when you explain them as 'just a joke.' "
- "Yes, salaried positions sometimes require working more than forty hours per week."
- "No, someone expressing a different opinion than yours is not the same as someone bullying you."
- "Yes, it is reasonable to expect you to show up to work as scheduled—you accepted the position and that is part of the job."

The list can go on and on.

If you are a person who has received management training, you've likely attended a practical Human Resources (HR) seminar, one that covers such socially awkward and legally dubious human behaviors. Unfortunately, these topics are rarely broken down into enough practical detail to be useful in the human conversations you need to have.[12]

---

12 HR's job is generally related to risk management, i.e., make sure the organization doesn't get sued. Discussing character can be surprising and feel a bit precarious—it is not a risk-free conversation. We are talking about it *here* to make it safer to talk about at work, so we can reinfuse humanity into our workplaces.

Most HR trainings are well-intentioned and focus on boilerplate messages that help your organization manage risk and the legal impact of workplace behaviors.[13] While necessary, this approach doesn't address our underlying assumptions about workplace behavior and doesn't help you to handle conversations in a language other than legalese. It's not how humans talk with each other outside of a courtroom.

Most unexpected conversations happen because we assume that people know what they're doing. We assume that everyone has the same awareness about what needs to be done and how to do it: a common understanding of terms like *work ethic* and *hard work*—and the expectation that you will hustle harder for recognition and success at work. The surprising conversations happen when we are gobsmacked or in a vulnerable position because our colleagues say or do something we aren't prepared for.

Here are a few examples of situations that can surprise the heck out of you:

- A client who has been shockingly rude to a coworker.
- A new-to-the-workplace colleague with little emotional self-regulation. Despite what can be inferred from TV shows and rom-coms, sobbing in front of clients when feeling stressed by deadlines is not a constructive approach.[14]
- Employees who do not know that running three months behind on all their projects isn't okay. Deadlines need to be met.
- Other unexpected topics and situations include:

---

13 HR also emphasizes fair employment practices, upholds Title VII of the Civil Rights Act of 1964, and helps to use the rule of law to create more equitable workplaces. In short: I'm a big fan.

14 When women cry at work, we are mocked as being too emotional. If men cry at work, they are labeled as weak. It's a ridiculous trap of shame and embarrassment. Everyone should be able to cry as needed. But at work and many social settings, emotional regulation and being able to speak *for* emotions—rather than being overwhelmed and speaking *from* them—is a powerful skill to develop. Unexpected and overt expression of emotion with actions like crying or yelling can be surprising to others as well as to yourself. It's the surprise and sense of being overwhelmed in an familiar situation (like a basic calendar meeting) that can cause communication problems, not the crying itself. See the References section for information on psychology and emotional health.

Having a hole in your aura is not necessarily a great reason to call out sick from work. Consider just calling out because you need the day to yourself.

- Having a hole in your aura is not necessarily a good reason to call out sick from work.
- Passing blame or feigning ignorance isn't a good look on anyone. Taking responsibility for one's own actions is important.
- Being the best producer on the team doesn't give an employee permission to be the biggest jerk.

- And when managing up (managing your boss) you may find yourself contemplating how to begin these types of conversations (ones you *really* wish you didn't need to have):
    - Making employees guess what you want is an unproductive leadership method.
    - The adage "being a boss means never having to say you're sorry" is not helpful for morale or business development
    - Intimidation and fear are not sustainable management tactics.

By the time you're done with this book, you will be able to think through these types of situations and know how to deal with them. You will also feel awkward or clumsy as you learn and experiment—that's part of getting good at anything.

ORIENTATION 19

If you dislike *not* being good at things immediately, or if your confidence is low due to the attitudes of the humans around you, don't despair. Remember: if you're going to add humanity back into how to work with humans, you must make the choice to practice something new. You can do it. Really.[15]

A Note About Practice: Sometimes You Mess Up

Practice is everything, and you will probably mess up from time to time. I have definitely missed the mark more than once. Like the time I accidentally insulted a lovely group of research librarians because I didn't check my assumptions first. It was the exact opposite of my awesome week with the educators at Harvard and the hoteliers in Vermont.

During a big project designed to help faculty understand the incredible value a team of research librarians can bring to academic work, an unexpected issue came up: due to a change in the phone system and confusion about which lines were which, no one in the research department was answering the phone when it rang. Faculty were annoyed and the research team were irritated with one another. It felt like everyone was expecting someone else to answer the phone and sort out the problem.

Confused by the situation, I asked bluntly, "How were you trained to answer the phone?" That one question projected a whole slew of assumptions from *my* experience in the hospitality industry onto *them*.[16]

Ten whip-smart people with two dozen advanced degrees between them stared at me in shock. The project lead looked at me, paused, and with razor-sharp politeness said, "I'm sorry, but I don't believe I understand your question."

---

15 And if you're eye-rolling at me so hard that you run the risk of spraining your face, that's okay, too. It's hard to take a risk and engage in something that makes you feel vulnerable without a clear, immediate payoff. Which is why I'm asking you to have a little faith in this work. Take a few deep breaths, and then do your First Assignment.

16 My assumption is this: no business phone should ring more than three times before it's answered. It doesn't matter if you work in that department or not. Say hello, thank them for calling, give them your name, and ask how you can help. Either put the caller on hold while you find someone who can answer their question or take a message. Answer. The. Phone. (So ends my sermon on phone etiquette.)

I tried to be more specific, unwittingly digging myself into a deeper hole, "When you started working here, how were you trained to answer the phone? How many times should a phone ring before you pick up, and what do you say when you answer?"

Librarians are not known to be violent people, but in the disdain-filled moments after I asked my questions, I suspected every person in that room was hoping an avalanche of the Oxford English Dictionary would engulf me right then and there.

"*Trained...?* Dogs are *trained*. We are professionals and educators. To reduce what we do to something that can be trained is insulting." The veins in her forehead became alarmingly visible.

Seeing the need for immediate clarification of my language choices, I explained.

"I apologize. I did not mean to insult your profession, your work, or the institution. I made a poor assumption about how your offices operate. I have a different set of experiences and assumptions about phones. It can be handy if everyone has the same frame of reference."

She sat back in her chair a fraction of an inch and nodded slightly; the room relaxed ever so slowly. I was spared the deluge of dictionaries. Had I used the tools you are going to learn at the start of that conversation, I would have avoided a relational mess with the people I was trying to help.

Your First Assignment:
How Do You Want to Feel at Work?

When we set out to fix a problem at work, all of our attention goes toward getting the problem to stop. We find a solution, apply it to that immediate situation, and move on. A short time later, when a similar problem pops up, we have a way to fix it: just apply our recent solution again. And again. And before we know it, we're playing Whack-a-Mole with workplace irritants.

We get stuck in this solution loop because we forget to think about what success looks like *beyond* fixing the problem.[17] What will that successful state feel like, and how will we recognize it when it happens? Note the word *feel*. Thinking is important, but for this assignment, focus on feeling. Knowing how you feel—in your body, heart, and spirit—is part of bringing humanity back into work, so that's where we'll start.

Read the following questions and let your mind wander a bit. Your responses may be short and succinct, or you may write paragraphs. Either is fine.

---

17 To learn more about how to incorporate Double Loop Learning, see Argyris, C. (1991). Teaching Smart People How to Learn. Harvard Business Review, 69(3), 99-109.

Recognize When Working With Humans Is *Working.*

Your responses should be specific enough that you notice how you feel, even if no one else does.

Take a few easy, slow breaths and let your mind relax. Then write down your answers.[18]

1. When I learn to communicate well, even in unexpected circumstances at work:

    - I will feel _____
      Examples: hopeful, more confident, less intimidated by Veronica in Accounts Payable
    - I will notice that I feel this way when I _____
      Examples: spend less time worrying about a conversation I had with my boss, am able to be clear with direction and timelines for my team, can talk calmly with Veronica when I spot an error on her weekly reports

2. When my coworkers and people I manage are doing better because communication and behavior have improved all around:

    - I will feel _____
      Examples: like we can be more effective as a team, that we like each other
    - I will notice this is happening when _____
      Examples: daily snarkiness decreases, people laugh more, I don't feel like I hate everyone I work with

---

[18] Try writing your responses by hand with pen and paper. Noticing how it feels to physically write is another way to bring your body into this activity.

3. Dream come true, at the end of a good day at work:
   - I will feel _____
   - When this happens, I will notice it because _____

   Examples: I will feel like I'm happier with my job because work is done without as much strain and nonsense. I will feel more at ease when I talk about my work with my friends and family.

After you've answered these questions, go for a walk or gaze up at the stars or lift weights or knit—something you enjoy that is not work-related. Then come back to your answers to see if they need modification or clarification. Adjust as needed. Keep these answers close. You'll come back to them later.

It may seem strange to daydream about answers to the questions above. It may feel precarious to be hopeful about what's possible. But without that vision of the future, that hope, we won't get very far. Hope is a form of planning.[19] It's the beginning of the structure of how we create change. Your hope and your vision are vital. Now, let's learn the tools that can make them real.

---

[19] Thank you, Gloria Steinem.

Learning About and Using Your Tools

CHARACTER COMPASS

NEEDED FOR EVERYTHING ELSE

TO BEGIN

YOU ARE IN SOME SORT OF SITUATION

abyss of cynicism

political quagmire

hard of fruitful effort

unicorn in a hay stack

USE & FINE TUNE YOUR CHARACTER COMPASS

NEED LEARNING, PRACTICE

PAUSE. BREATHE. YOU ARE GOING TO MAKE IT THROUGH.

YOU ARE HERE

YOUR ESSENTIAL TOOLS

CHARACTER COMPASS
- KEY BEHAVIORS
- COMMUNICATION
- CONTEXT

WHACK A MOLE!

THIS IS YOUR FOUNDATION, YOUR GUIDE

COMPASS IS USED FROM HERE ON OUT

your **CHARACTER** = $\dfrac{\text{VALUES ENACTED}}{\text{TIME}}$ *over*

TOO M OF ANY THESE IS NEEDS BALAN TO WO

YOU ARE RESPONSIBLE FOR YOUR OWN CHARACTER & BEHAVIOR

moral quicksand

ego cliffs

caution long way down

** WE ASSUME WE KNOW WHAT THIS IS... BUT WE DON'T OFTEN CHECK TO SEE IF WE ARE CORRECT

HOPES

Your Character Compass

> "But there are no new ideas still waiting in the wings to save us as women, as humans. There are only old and forgotten ones, new combinations, extrapolations and recognitions from within ourselves, along with the renewed courage to try them out." —Audre Lorde

Essential Tool #1: Your Character Compass

Character is the most important and most under-appreciated tool at work.

There are many meanings of the word, all of which have practical uses. They include the following:

- A fictional person represented in a film, play, or novel
- A quirky individual: "he's quite a character"
- A symbol in a writing system, such as letters in an alphabet
- The complex mental and ethical traits marking and often individualizing a person

When we talk about character in this book, we're using the last of those definitions, and it is anchored in our relationship to ourselves and others.

Character is developed by enacting your values consistently, over time.

Character is the anchor for all of the risks you're going to take while learning how to use the tools in this book. Many challenges at work can be alleviated when we can talk about the values that influence our choices and behaviors. When you know how to perceive and talk about your own values and use them intentionally, you gain confidence in your own abilities and can feel very grounded in how you work and connect with others.

∞

With most any topic or circumstance, it's the personal experience and character of a conversation that matters most when working with humans. You and a colleague may share an interest in quantum physics, but if she is dismissive and rude to you every time you strike up a conversation, it doesn't matter if she's a perfect match to your intellect—who wants to chat with a jerk? Conversely, you may disagree about who should win *Dancing with the Stars* or the World Cup, but if your debate is respectful and appreciative of your shared love of the event, you can argue vigorously and still have a great interaction. In either case, the underlying qualities of character that you bring to the conversation are what stabilize and contextualize the interaction overall.

Qualities of character—the values you use to make choices—are the bedrock of everything you do at work. They are your touchstone for every choice you make. The importance of character is a millennia-old idea, but we don't talk about it much. It's a topic made of timeless ingredients that require reflection. Character is often left out of conversations about what it means to be successful. It's not flashy, quantifiable, or easily obtained, but it's part of what makes working with others easier. Talking about character is something we need to do with purpose because it's good for us—kind of like making time to exercise, eating our vegetables, and getting enough sleep. None of those things are revolutionary but, without them, the revolution is way harder than it needs to be.

Have you ever heard the word *values* at work and thought, "Yikes! Talking about values at work? No, thank you." Certainly when "values" are wielded with loaded meanings, we should question how the word is being used; examples include:

- "Family values"—a term that leaves a lot of opportunity for political or religious meanings to be inferred. This is heavy-handed and exclusionary.
- The corporate "Values Statement"—frequently *BORing* (and often inconsequential if not used within the context of behavior and operational decisions)
- As a verb: *Shawna values her job.* It's important to notice the opportunities and experiences that we find important in our lives.

Each of these is worth recognizing. But what you need as a baseline for becoming a superstar communicator at work is to know and use your values practically and in real-time at work. That's why we ground them in the context of character. That's the game-changer other values exercises skip. It's what I call your Character Compass.

If character is so good for us, why have we forgotten to include it when we work with humans? Because the business of productivity works faster without it. When doing more, being the best, and hitting all your targets is the principal focus of work, there is little time to discuss the manner in which we do those things. The "manner in which" we do things is where we can infuse our actions with humanity and care. It's the sweet spot in working with humans. Without character, you can become removed from the value of your work, and that can break your spirit. Character is one of the three Essential Tools because, when you operate without it, work can feel horrible. And you may, too.

Fortunately, once you explore your own character and talk about its importance with others, you quickly become aware of its importance in all you do. It may feel like coming home, or like articulating something you've needed but haven't known how to talk about. It's the essential basis of getting good at working with humans, which is why we look at it first.

Your Character Compass helps you use your values in a practical manner to work better with humans every day. Yes, it's a commitment to accept this kind of responsibility for yourself. It requires effort. All good things do. It requires you to pay attention to yourself and your effect on those around you. It's also totally badass because most people avoid doing it. Which means you can excel in ways you can't yet imagine.

As you continue to use your Character Compass, you'll notice you gain calm confidence in those surprising conversations that used to throw you off or shut you down. Other people will notice, too. That will build your reputation as a person who knows themself well and is consistent in how they treat others. People will want to know how you are able to communicate so well in so many unexpected and awkward moments. You will tell them it's because you know who you are and what you value—that you make choices that are true to your character. It's a great feeling. Let's take a look.

Your Second Assignment:
Make Your Character Compass

Moral philosophers would describe character with greater detail and nuance, but in general terms: character is developed by enacting your values consistently, over time. Character builds on itself. The more you work on it, the more resilient it can become.

Character Compass | Step One:

Below is a long list of qualities that contribute to creating character. Circle the ten that are most meaningful to you. These can be qualities you value in yourself, that are inspired by others, or some combination of both. We all use all of these qualities, so circle the ones that resonate most for you.

Accomplishment	Communication	Effectiveness	Hope
Accountability	Community	Empathy	Humility
Adaptability	Compassion	Endurance	Humor
Altruism	Competence	Energy	Imagination
Ambition	Confidence	Enthusiasm	Independence
Assertiveness	Connection	Excellence	Individuality
Attentiveness	Consistency	Experience	Insight
Awareness	Contentment	Fairness	Integrity
Balance	Conviction	Fidelity	Intelligence
Beauty	Cooperation	Foresight	Intuition
Boldness	Courage	Fortitude	Irreverence
Bravery	Courtesy	Friendship	Joy
Brilliance	Creativity	Fun	Justice
Calmness	Curiosity	Generosity	Kindness
Certainty	Decisiveness	Grace	Knowledge
Charity	Dependability	Gratitude	Lawfulness
Clarity	Determination	Growth	Leadership
Cleverness	Devotion	Happiness	Learning
Commitment	Dignity	Honesty	Liberty
Common sense	Discipline	Honor	Logic

Love	Presence	Significance	Thoroughness
Loyalty	Prosperity	Simplicity	Thoughtfulness
Mastery	Purpose	Sincerity	Tolerance
Meaning	Quality	Skillfulness	Trust
Moderation	Reason	Smarts	Truthfulness
Motivation	Recognition	Solitude	Understanding
Openness	Recreation	Spirituality	Uniqueness
Optimism	Respect	Stability	Unity
Order	Responsibility	Status	Valor
Originality	Reverence	Stewardship	Vigor
Passion	Rigor	Strength	Vision
Patience	Risk	Structure	Vitality
Peace	Security	Success	Wisdom
Perseverance	Self-reliance	Support	Wonder
Persistence	Selflessness	Sustainability	
Playfulness	Sensitivity	Teamwork	Additional
Poise	Serenity	Temperance	qualities:
Potential	Service	Tenacity	_____
Power	Sharing	Thankfulness	_____

Character Compass | Step Two:

Look at the ten qualities you circled that contribute to character. Are some more important than others? Do some of them build off each other or offer sharp contrast to each other? Bring some curiosity to the values and behaviors you find meaningful in your own life and reflect on the ways each one influences your choices and actions during the differing circumstances of daily life.

Prioritize your list in the space below. Is there one quality that is most important to you? Are there a few that are the key drivers in your life? A few that you'd like to emphasize more? Write them down and then see which of them keep drawing your attention.

1	6
2	7
3	8
4	9
5	10

TOP 4

Character Compass | Step Three:

From your list of ten, choose the four qualities that are the most important to YOU. They may be different from what other people or influences in your life expect them to be. These are the qualities you feel most drawn to in EVERY situation: personal, professional, social, financial, etc. (Why only four? It makes remembering them easier!)

These qualities of character are now your compass headings—your touchstones for navigating the world and how you work with humans.

This compass is a tool to help you make values-informed choices and develop the character you want to have as you navigate the world and your experiences within it.

When you make choices, ask yourself if they align with your compass headings. If they do, carry on. If they don't, ask yourself: why not? They may be misaligned with your values. Making choices that are rooted in your character makes working with humans easier.

Using and Fine-Tuning Your Character Compass

The key to getting the Character Compass to work for you is to use it regularly and refine it as you go so it becomes integrated into how you work with humans. This is not a performative exercise you do once and forget about. It's a functional tool that's always with you.

When selecting and then refining your Character Compass headings, take your time as you consider which ones feel best. This can seem a little daunting because we use all of the 150 qualities of character listed at one time or another. So, how do you know the qualities that work best to you?

First and foremost, examine your influences. Think of the people or institutions that helped form and cultivate the values that feel most true to you, such as:

- Parents and family
- Friends
- Fictional characters[20]
- Religions
- Schools
- Social groups
- Political parties
- National identity

Do those who have influenced you maintain values that may be useful for others but don't honestly fit for you?

If you were raised in a religion that upheld reverence as the way to honor the sacred, you may expect reverence to be an important value on your compass. Or you may not.

I encourage you to notice that reverence is something you were taught to uphold and then ask yourself whether it is important enough to the person you are now to be one of your main Character Compass points.

---

20 Some of the most influential people in my life are characters from books and movies: Rosalind Russell's *Auntie Mame*, Cary Grant's C.K. Dexter Haven in *The Philadelphia Story* (actually, every character in that movie), and Kay Thomson and Hillary Knight's *Eloise*. They have served me well and supported me with the values of courage, playfulness, curiosity, and sheer chutzpah.

You may determine that, yes, reverence is an external influence from your religious upbringing and something you use to determine your best choices now. You may also discover that it is no longer a primary driver for you. Instead, you may choose calmness, patience, fairness, or thoughtfulness. Each of these values can be used to show respect and love for what you hold sacred.

The key is to notice if the values you are selecting are true to you and your own heart now, or if they are values you're using because you are "supposed" to, or if they fit an older version of you. This distinction can take time to sort out.

> Your compass is not meant to be used as an objectivist, ego-centric way of saying, "I value these things so I don't have to do things your way. I'm following my values, so y'all can shove it." Seeing your influences helps you identify and honor which values are yours and why. It also allows you to gain a depth of understanding about the values of others.

One challenge people deal with in choosing the top four values on their Character Compass is that some values are closely connected and are often used interchangeably. At the same time, similar qualities can also be expressed very differently. If you get stuck while narrowing down your choices, think about your top four values as access points to related values.

For example, one of my four Character Compass points is kindness. I chose it after thinking about values on my top ten list that were related to kindness. My top ten included compassion, love, and helpfulness.[21] I ended up choosing kindness as a compass point because it assists me in

---

21 Being *kind* is not the same as being *nice*. Nice is pablum, a veneer of pleasantries that are sometimes needed but do not develop your character. Sometimes the kindest thing you can do for someone is not necessarily the thing that is nice: "OMG, dude. You have toilet paper stuck to your shoe and you walked through the whole restaurant that way when you came back from the restroom…"

choosing *how* I show love, compassion, and helpfulness—an example of how one value can be an access point for others. Kindness is the value I lead with when I consider ways in which I want to be helpful. If I were to dash around inflicting helpfulness on clients, which *gulp* I admit I have done (unintentionally) from time to time, I would not necessarily be kind. In fact, I could end up being controlling, enabling, or even rude. When I connect to my Character Compass and the value of kindness, I am more thoughtful and aware of my actions and the ways in which I can be of help.

Deciding which values will be your access points can take a little time and require some reflection and clear definitions of the values you choose, especially if you select values that are interrelated. For example, patience, presence, and thoughtfulness are three values that are sometimes considered similar. In Western culture, it's common to use these words interchangeably to point to ideas of being mindful or calmly reflective about what we say and do. Consider how these three values support each other:

- Patience may be seen as a way of demonstrating your thoughtfulness.
  - If you are working with someone who is struggling to learn a new skill, you may recognize your desire to be *thoughtful* as they learn and to communicate in a *patient* way that respects their need for time to process new information.
- Or you may wish to show that you are *present* to a situation–openhearted and awake to the moment–by being thoughtful and patient.
- Which of those words would be the handiest access point for you on a daily basis?
- Take time to consider whether one value seems like it is the overarching theme of the others.
  - There is no right answer—the value just has to make sense for you and how you will use it in your Character Compass.

Another good indicator of whether a value is a solid choice for you is if you can apply it to yourself and to others. Kindness is that way for me. I value being kind to myself—in my thoughts, feelings, and actions—and I value being kind to others. If I had a value that I could only use for

Keep Refining Your Character Compass

This may take some time and experimentation

- Perhaps you had both *friendship* and *generosity* in your top ten. As you begin to pay attention to both, one may become more significant. You might think, "I noticed that, for me, the basis of friendship is generosity: a willingness to give of oneself and share one's spirit. That's why generosity is one of my Character Compass headings."
  - Generosity becomes one of the values on your Character Compass
  - Continue to reflect on your list and refine your top ten down to your top four. You can have more or fewer if you wish, but four points map nicely to the points on a magnetic compass.
- Practice using each of your top four values throughout every day
  - Let's say your values are *tenacity*, *structure*, *clarity*, and *courtesy*.
  - When you go into a meeting, ask yourself, "How can I contribute to or ask for clarity in this group?" or "How can I model courtesy even if others have no idea what it is?"
- Ask yourself: what are the influences behind this compass heading?
  - Influences can be good. But identify what your influences are and whether they support you and your character development or the norms of a group.
  - Examine and evaluate which values steer your choices and most clearly resonate with who you are at your core—and which values are congruent with who you are becoming.

others but not for myself, that would not be a good Character Compass heading. For example, if I said that I am amazed by the quality of endurance in other people—their ability to withstand anything that the world throws their way—but I did not value that in myself, then endurance wouldn't be a good choice for my Character Compass.

Choosing Your Character Compass Points

The values that you choose for your Character Compass may feel obvious to you. "Yep, dignity. That's clearly one of my values." Or they can be values you're striving to include in your daily life—but be careful about this approach. Sometimes we choose values because we think we are *supposed* to. That's a red flag because that value doesn't resonate with you but with your community, family, or the dominant culture.

It's one thing to say to yourself, "I appreciate and admire generosity in the world, and I notice that my life is fuller when I am in touch with the value of generosity. It's important to me and I want it to guide more of my choices," versus saying, "I'm supposed to be generous because at church I learned that 'It is more blessed to give than to receive,' so I'm going to pick generosity as a Character Compass point because that's what I should do. It makes me a good person."

Beware of "should" when choosing your values. The word "should" is often fraught with judgment. If you find yourself choosing Character Compass headings that are aspirational—what you think "good people" should choose—pull the handbrake on this exercise.

You will know the values you have chosen for your Character Compass are right for you when they give you a sense of easy knowing and clear resonance about your choices. Your Character Compass aligns your thoughts, words, and choices in a way that feels obvious, natural, and startlingly good.

Character in Action

Let's move into action. Start practicing using your Character Compass by choosing the value that's easiest, most comfortable, or makes you feel good. This will help you experience how powerful your Character Compass can be. Don't start by practicing the value that is most challenging for you—there is no prize for doing the hardest thing first. It's okay to practice and get a handle on things to gain confidence. Starting with your most challenging values may make you lose confidence or doubt your skill with this tool. I want you to set yourself up for success.

One of my Character Compass values is joy. In today's world of political strife, global pandemic, human rights violations, climate change, and economic confusion, it can be hard to find a sense of joy. But it's a value that helps me make good decisions, share my love of this frustrating and glorious world, and celebrate the delight that surrounds us every day. Joy is a wonderful way to connect with the humanity of others.

When joy feels a little out of reach, I don't let that dissuade me from using my Character Compass. Instead, I go to another value on my Compass: curiosity. I can *always* ask a question. I can *always* find something to wonder about, something I don't know. Once I feel connected to curiosity and hang out there a bit, I can find kindness. Then, when I'm grounded in those values, I can connect to joy.

The point of having and using your Character Compass is not to judge yourself in the face of a challenging situation. *The point is to be able to remember who you are and what matters to you, then use that information to make good choices that continue to develop your character.* This tool isn't meant to be a burden, it's meant to be a guide and a source of calm and support.

Some more questions to consider while creating your Character Compass:

1. Where do you struggle?
   - Let's say you wrestle with persistence or humility. *When do you notice this struggle? In what situations?*
2. What concern underlies that struggle?
   - In this example, it may be fear, uncertainty, or timidity. If so, the value you need to tap into may not be persistence or humility, but courage, confidence, or tenacity. Any of these values may support your ability to manage your underlying concerns and take action.
3. What actions are important to you in the world?
   - Look at the people you admire. They often have qualities of character you value deeply. You may find that the values you appreciate are ones you have within you but don't notice you are using.

Remember: *Character is developed by enacting your values consistently, over time.*

---

4. What are you supposed to love or respect but just don't?
   - For example: In my work in business, I am supposed to value productivity. It has its place, but it can chafe my spirit. I think it hyper-fixates people on seeing their value only as output-generators and on attaching to productivity for its own sake–which can further alienate us from our humanity. Instead, I'm a fan of *fruitfulness*. Being fruitful is creative, worthy of sustained effort, and is very playful. It gets me out of the trap of being busy for no clear purpose. Being fruitful is delicious.

5. What do you long for?
   - In your heart of hearts, what are your hopes for yourself and the world? What is the manner in which you would most like to bring your dream about?
6. Who are the people you most admire and what do you admire about them?
   - Make a list of these people and the qualities they represent to you.
   - Do you see any values reflected in what you admire or what they represent?
7. If you were known for one value on the list, what would it be?
   - That is a strong indicator of one of your Character Compass headings.

Keep Practicing

The words you listed as your top ten and the ones you chose for your Character Compass points are important to you and, hopefully, are good for you, too. But there can be too much or too little of a good thing. Aristotle (384-322 BCE) believed that character could be developed with effort and attention. His table of virtues and vices shows how even the best qualities of character can be problematic in their extreme forms. He strove for the mean, the middle balance, where each quality works and feels best.

As you continue to practice with your Character Compass, look to see if any of your chosen qualities align with the mean, below. These are qualities that many people associate with character, even when they use complementary words to describe them. Being able to recognize where your values connect to, complement, or contrast with the values of others can be a handy anchor for better conversation as you work with humans.

Aristotle's Table of Virtues and Vices:

SPHERE OF ACTION OR FEELING	EXCESS	MEAN	DEFICIENCY
Fear and Confidence	Rashness	**Courage**	Cowardice
Pleasure and Pain	Licentiousness/ Self-indulgence	**Temperance**	Insensibility
Getting and Spending (minor)	Prodigality	**Liberality**	Illiberality/ Meanness
Getting and Spending (major)	Vulgarity/ Tastelessness	**Magnificence**	Pettiness/ Stinginess
Honor and Dishonor (major)	Vanity	**Magnanimity**	Pusillanimity
Honor and Dishonor (minor)	Ambition/ Empty vanity	**Proper ambition/Pride**	Unambitiousness/ Undue humility
Anger	Irascibility	**Patience/ Good temper**	Lack of spirit/ Unirascibility
Self-expression	Boastfulness	**Truthfulness**	Understatement/ Mock modesty
Conversation	Buffoonery	**Wittiness**	Boorishness
Social Conduct	Obsequiousness	**Friendliness**	Cantankerousness
Shame	Shyness	**Modesty**	Shamelessness
Indignation	Envy	**Righteous indignation**	Malicious enjoyment/ Spitefulness

Aristotle. The Ethics of Aristotle: The Nicomachean Ethics. (rev. ed.) (J. K. Thomson, trans.). New York: Viking, 1955.

"It is no mean happiness, therefore, to be seated in the mean."

Nerissa to Portia, William Shakespeare, *Merchant of Venice* (1.2.7-8)

Character | Common Uses

Use your Character Compass in real-time. A good way to know if you need to check in with your Compass is if you find yourself asking questions like:
- "How do I tell him that we have to move him to a new department?"
- "How do I figure out who to assign to this project?"
- "I don't want my peers to think I'm stepping on their toes. How can I offer help without offending them?"
- "What am I going to do? Whatever choice I make, someone is going to be upset."
- "Why should I have to explain this again?! Don't they know why this is important?"
- "How can I stand up for my team in a way I feel proud of while redirecting this bullying client to knock-it-the-eff-off?"

These are the types of questions we ask ourselves all the time. This is true whether we are managing only ourselves (the most vital and effective place to start), managing a group, a project, or an entire company. At first glance, these questions seem to be about process, the sequence of steps to take to get something done. But re-read the questions. Is there an unspoken concern or emotional undercurrent in there?

Once you have chosen the values for your Character Compass, you will notice that when you ask, "How am I going to ___," you're really asking, "How can I do this in a way that is aligned with my character?"

When we talk about character, *how* has to do with the *manner in which* you do something, not the method. Here's an example to show you what I mean.

Using your Character Compass

Dave was a new manager in a department that uses temporary contract employees for short sprints of work, four to six weeks at a time. He realized that the project a well-qualified temp had been working on was going to end after four weeks rather than six. Dave liked this temporary employee and valued her work, but wasn't feeling confident about telling her that her work was ending sooner rather than later, even though that possibility was in her work agreement.

In an online coaching session, he asked me, "How do I tell her that we must end her contract? I need to tell her tomorrow that she'll be done by the end of next week."

I knew that he was not asking a method question—about the step-by-step process of speaking to her—so I asked, "What's your concern about telling her?"

"That she'll think we're bad employers who are yanking her around, and that she'll never want to temp for us again. I don't want that; she's good!"

"Okay, what are the qualities of character you bring to this conversation? What are your Character Compass headings?"

He took a breath as he remembered, "Generosity, integrity, learning, and patience."

"Great. Given that you do need to end her contract, how can you uphold each of those in the conversation? Walk me through each one."

"Generosity: I can thank her for the quality of her work. I can be generous in sharing positive feedback. I can tell her I'd like to keep her at the top of the list for the support we will need in the spring." I saw his posture relax as he described how his values would connect to his actions.

"Integrity: I want to uphold the contract. I also want to be true to the fact that I wish we could have her here longer. I can be respectful about the terms of employment and how much I've appreciated working with her.

"Learning: I'm learning how to do this. I want to ask her if the temp contracts are clear enough or if there is anything that would make them clearer in the future. I also want to learn whether she's willing to work with us again.

"Patience: I need to have patience with myself when I get nervous about how to talk with people about hard things." He smiled as he realized what this conversation had done for his patience.

I was glad to see his relief and smiled back at him through the ether and a computer screen. "Given all of that, how are you going to tell her? What are your next steps?"

Dave said, "I'll tell her at our weekly check-in that her contract will be ending at the end of next week, that I really value her work, and that it's been a pleasure to work with her. I'll ask her if she'd be willing to work here again and if there is anything she needs next week to wrap up her work. I'm going to be respectful and open—and patient with myself as I listen to her."

Dave reported to me that the conversation went well. Because he oriented himself to his Character Compass, he was more confident and at ease rather than gummed-up by the unpredictability of his worry. He knew what he wanted to say, and he knew *how* he wanted to say it.

People can sense when you are present and anchored to your character. If you are clear within yourself before you open your mouth, it calms your anxiety about what you need to say. **Your character gets you through.**

Unexpected Conversations:
Character

Unexpected conversations are ones where the content, circumstance, or timing surprises you. Remember, being human at work means learning to handle these conversations and to grow because of them, rather than avoid them in the name of productivity. The single handiest tool you have in navigating the unexpected is your Character Compass.

Think back to a conversation you've had at work recently. Maybe you had to ask your colleagues to stop taking your food from the fridge. Maybe, if you are managing others, you had to point out to seasoned employees that new hires were being excluded from trivia night. Reflect on how and whether the values on your Character Compass showed up in these conversations. Don't fret if you forgot to use the tool—it's still worthwhile to reflect. If you had brought more of a particular value into the conversation, do you think it might have gone differently? Or felt different to you?

When you plan for a conversation in the future—even if it's not a surprising conversation (easy conversations are the best place to practice!)—pause to check in with your Character Compass first so you feel grounded in your character.

Think of the questions people spring on you and the circumstances you must respond to on the fly. Examples include:
- Handling an unexpected client request
- Addressing a coworker's sexist or racist remarks
- Responding to an employee when they give their notice
- Learning that a coworker is going to be out on leave longer than expected and you need to distribute their workload to others on your team while still keeping on top of your own

More Examples:

For yourself: In each of these situations, breathe and think of the Character Compass point that feels easiest to use in that moment. Then, respond in a way that is consistent with that quality.

When managing others: Connect to your Character Compass before you talk with the people you are managing. Think about which of your Character Compass qualities will support the conversations you need to have—whether you are giving annual reviews or dealing with an immediate crisis. As you begin addressing topics with the people you manage, speak in a way that feels steady and grounded in your qualities of character.

When you find yourself in an unexpected conversation, know that you do not need to know what to do or how to respond that *instant*. The pressure of productivity and its associated sense of speed is problematic for skills development.

Here's what to do instead, and this takes less than a minute. That minute is worth its weight in platinum because it saves you time and energy in the long run:

1. Take a breath to slow yourself down.
2. Say, "Let me think about that for a moment." Keep breathing… inhale, exhale… repeat *(it's the repeating part that's important)*.
3. While you're breathing, connect to your Character Compass in your mind's eye. Which quality is easiest to use in this moment? Pick that one and then start the conversation in a way that feels true to that quality.

    - Connecting to your values helps you feel more comfortable when surprising circumstances and conversations occur. Your Character Compass helps you make choices and have conversations in a grounded, reliable way.

In all you do at work, unexpected or planned, start by connecting to your Character Compass. Everything becomes easier.

Practice With a Pal:
Character

Practice, practice, practice

1. Find a pal at work. *A pal is someone worthy of your trust, open to direct and meaningful discussion of topics, and who supports your learning and development as a person.* If you don't have a pal at work, that's a bummer, but it's okay. Just find a person in your life who is open to talking about things other than the weather (heck, strike up a conversation on the bus or with your postal carrier if that feels easier).

   - Tell your pal that you are working on developing your communication skills and need their help. You want to talk about the qualities of character most of us take for granted in day-to-day life.

     They may look a little surprised because it's not a common topic of conversation—fear not! We need to make these conversations normal if we are going to acknowledge the humanity in our workplaces.

2. Set aside some time—ten to twenty minutes—to talk about the qualities of character you find most meaningful.

   - Before you meet, reflect on your own Character Compass headings. Pick one and start the conversation with these questions:
     - *What's your definition of /what comes to mind when you think of this quality?*
     - *How do you notice it in others? What are they doing that demonstrates this quality?*
     - *For extra fun: have your friend draw an image of this quality in action.*[22]
     - *When do you see this at work?*
   - Listen to your pal's answers and then ask them to listen as you answer the same questions.

---

22 Gray, Dave., Brown, Sunni., Macanufo, James. Gamestorming: A Playbook for Innovators, Rulebreakers, and Changemakers. Japan: O'Reilly Media, 2010. Try the game called Graphic Jam.

- Then, discuss your answers:
  - *How are your answers similar?*
  - *How are they different?*
  - *Do your responses complement each other? Contradict? Do they provide a more well-rounded definition of the quality? Do they help you know your pal better?*
- Do this for the other values on your Character Compass.
- This discussion allows you to understand each other more fully and to talk about a topic—values—in a neutral way that brings open-hearted curiosity into the conversation.
- If you're up for it, here are a couple of questions to continue the conversation:
  - *What's the one quality of character you want to be known for, and why?*
  - *Who are your heroes, and why?*

With each of these questions and answers, listen deeply.[23] Your replies and definitions will both contrast and complement each other. The point is to start practicing the discussion of values and qualities of character.

Bonus Activity:
These are the kind of conversations we need to be having about politics. Can you bring your character with you into a topic where you and your pal have different political perspectives? If you orient yourself to the conversation using your Character Compass before you begin, what happens as you talk? Can you listen differently? Can you hear the values the other person is trying to describe when they express a difference?

Even if you cannot discuss politics with people who think and feel differently than you do, you can listen and identify the values and qualities of character that are important in someone else's opinion. We must find the courage to recognize and make use of the qualities we share if we are to salvage our communities and national landscape from the perils of polarization.

---

23 Listening "is an *art* like the understanding of poetry." Fromm, Erich. The Art of Listening. United States: Open Road Media, 2013.

Signs Character is helping and attuned:	Signs Character needs some attention:
Feeling more confident about your choices.	Second-guessing your choices and not trusting yourself.
Can easily describe your choices and thinking if asked.	Feeling defensive about your actions even if no one is asking for information or questioning you.
Background anxiety about work and colleagues quiets.	Anxiety, imposter syndrome, and hurriedness increase; often feeling unprepared or behind.
Feeling physically balanced, like your center of gravity is lower; deeper breathing; ability to be responsive and flexible.	Feeling detrimentally hyper-focused or hyper-confident; off balance; clenched muscles.
Ready to handle the next task at hand.	Disinterested and apathetic... *whatever...*

Practice with a pal

What's in It for YOU
and how do you know if it's working?

Checking for Character and Adjusting as Needed

How do you know if your Character Compass is working for you? I'd love to hand you a physical compass that magically attunes to your desired qualities of character. Then you could use it automatically anytime you wanted a nudge toward the direction of your values.

Alas, you're going to have to do this calibration yourself—by observing how you *want* to feel versus how you *actually* feel after a conversation and then comparing those feelings to your compass headings.

When you're wondering if using your values is helping you work with humans, do the following:

1. Take a slow, easy breath.[24] Deliberate, unhurried reflection is an element of weaving humanity into our workplaces. It's easy to skip and *vital* to practice.
2. Reread your responses to the questions in the first assignment in the Orientation chapter.
   - Those responses help you stay on track and get better at working with humans.
   - Examine and evaluate them.

When you connect to your qualities of character often and use them to make communication choices, you'll likely feel more at ease and satisfied.[25] That can feel different to every person, but the common thing people report is a sense of clarity—like there isn't extra noise or static when communicating. When your Character Compass is attuned and you're using it well, you may feel quiet and relaxed, or you may feel like

---

[24] You've probably noticed by now that I tell you to pause and breathe a lot. That's because, in the span of a single, deep, intentional breath, you can steady your nervous system, increase your oxygen levels, and help your brain function better. It also gives you the gift of time. The moments you give to yourself are gifts to your own humanity.

[25] It may also feel a little uncomfortable. If you have been doing things that conflict with your values, the recalibration to your Character Compass can be tricky and demand a lot of effort. Keep at it.

you want to sing at the top of your lungs because you're so thrilled. The thing you won't feel is that it's all bullshit. You may have a habitual voice in your head telling you character isn't important, or that you should use the values that other people use to know what to say next, but your body and your spirit will know that's not true. Trust yourself. Remember that you're connecting to humanity and you, dear reader, are a human. You may just need some practice with these basics.

If you find that you're not sure if you're "doing it right" and feel many of the things on the right side of the table above, that's okay. Keep practicing using your Character Compass in different situations. If you don't have a lot of experience attuning your choices to the qualities of character that are most important to you, it may take a while to get the hang of it.

If you notice, however, that it doesn't feel quite right to make a choice from, say, *tenacity* but that *adaptability* is what you were after, great! Change your compass heading and practice from there.

Your Character Compass is *yours*. It must resonate with you and help you discern how best to work with humans.

A note: You need to do the exercises in this book. I'm not kidding. Don't wing it. Do the First Assignment, make your Character Compass, and Practice With a Pal. That's how we figure this stuff out. I told you this was difficult and boring and occasionally awkward. I hope that attending to the simple and seemingly commonplace elements of knowing and openly talking about your character is piquing your interest, and that you're starting to see that the effort is worth it.

In summary, what's in it for you is this:

When you know your character and you can use it well, it becomes a tool for discernment that will help you feel steady in a world that often feels unstable.

Your character helps you navigate all the weird stuff that work will throw at you. It helps you make decisions that you feel proud of, even when they are difficult. It enables you to bring consistency and reliability to how you engage with yourself and others. It decreases the noise of other people's opinions and helps you stay true to your spirit.

COMMUNICATION MUST HAVES:

REQUIRES CONSTANT CALIBRATION

CORE QUESTIONS:

WHY ♥

WHAT !

waterfall of hope

HOW →

IF 👁

4 THINGS TO DO FOREVER

1. COMMUNICATE CLEARLY
2. SET EXPECTATIONS
3. GET COMMITMENT
4. FOLLOW THROUGH

PRACTICE WITH A PAL

EXPECTATIONS INVENTORY

WACK-A-MOLE!

TOO MUCH OF ANY OF THESE IS BAD. NEEDS BALANCE TO WORK.

soft knees, drink water.

navigate core questions

caution long way

MAGIC ANSWER

The Communication Must-Haves

Essential Tool #2:
The Communication Must-Haves

How many times have you had a conversation where you thought you knew what you'd agreed upon, only to have the other person do something else entirely? Or nothing at all?

Miscommunication and misunderstanding are the sources of infinite irritations in the workplace, ranging from client contract disputes to people being perpetually late to meetings to whether the heating and cooling system works. *99% of all problems at work are because of problems in our communication.*

Communicating well is not brain surgery, rocket science, *or* rocket surgery—though it's essential to all three. The problem is that most of us are not taught how to communicate well. You know this. That's why you're reading this book. You can't help but wonder: if this happens every day, shouldn't we have managed to fix our communication issues by now?

Humans are born communicators—the gift of language is inherent, it's part of what makes us human, and we take being able to use it for granted. We connect through language, symbols, motion, and sound so automatically that we overlook two big challenges:

1. Ability does not necessarily equate to skill.
2. People can talk *around* almost any subject to avoid interpersonal conflict—otherwise known as the conversations you never expected to have.

Which is why we mess it up. We *can* communicate—and we do: all day, every day—so we assume that, since it's so common, everyone will be able to do it *well*. We can also move our bodies, add numbers together, and place words into sentences; but that doesn't automatically make us the next Simone Biles, Stephen Hawking, or Maya Angelou.[26] We have a cultural understanding that certain things take practice, patience, and persistence to do well. We don't have that same understanding about communication—but we should.

The weird thing is that when you are learning to do something specific like gymnastics, math, or writing, you learn how to improve your performance by *communicating* about it. Communication is both its own skill and how we learn and share information and meaning. The irony is that we aren't taught how to do the thing—communication—that helps us get better at everything else. Weird, right?

∞

---

26 Simone Biles is the most decorated American gymnast in history and the recipient of numerous prestigious awards for her athleticism and leadership. Stephen Hawking was a famed British professor, scientist, and author known for his work in physics and cosmology and for making science more accessible to everyone. Maya Angelou was an activist, poet, singer, dancer, and world-renowned author, best known for her autobiographical writing style.

When I started my management consulting business, I knew why I wanted to focus on communication: it is the skill most managers and leaders desperately need to develop and its absence is what gums-up the works in every type of organization, making it hard to do the work you were hired to do. I knew this was true from my professional experience, my academic study, and from my daily observations of how easy it is for bad communication to make good humans miserable. But even knowing all this, as I began to launch my consulting company, there was an itch at the back of my memory, just beyond my awareness, a longing to understand why this communication work was so important.

One gray and cozy fall morning during the first year of my business, I awoke with vivid dreamscape depictions of Diego Rivera's mural *Detroit Industry* swirling through my mind. In a flash, I felt a wave of clarity and gratitude. My subconscious had given my memory the shove it needed: the entirety of the Rivera Courtyard, including those famous murals, is the perfect representation of how people communicate when we work together.

Diego Rivera, *Detroit Industry, North Wall*, 1932-1933, Fresco, Detroit Institute of Art, Detroit, Michigan.

I remember being mesmerized by those images as a kid in Detroit. When I was little, I didn't care about the political themes or the science-versus-religion debate that made the murals so intensely scrutinized when they were commissioned during the Great Depression. What I was drawn to was the idea that there was so much involved for each person to do their work—the murals are maps of our interconnectedness. I sensed in Rivera's paintings that I could always learn something more about how people worked together. Yes, you can view the metal and the fuel and the effort and the enormity of the setting as a warning of the dangers of productivity. That's part of the story, but it's the *people* in the painting—their strength, their gracefully mirrored movements, their intelligence and skill, their focus, their mythic presence, their cooperation—that is human. That is art—and how we communicate about it feels magical to me.

Let's explore two sets of tools that will help you get better at the skill that makes that magic possible.

There are two important qualities you must use to be able to communicate well:

#1: Curiosity—about yourself and others
#2: Clarity—willingness to use your curiosity and intuition for understanding

Quick reminder: Keep your Character Compass with you! It will come in handy.

Core Questions—
Curiosity Starts Here

> "I know you believe that you understand what you think I said, but I am not sure you realize that what you heard is not what I meant." – *Robert McCloskey*

Have you ever noticed that the same group of people can attend the same meeting, yet each person will understand what was said differently? Ever tried to teach a friend something like how to throw a baseball or how to make gravy and they seem mostly tuned-out until suddenly they perk up and get what you've been explaining? What people pay attention to and how you prefer to explain things are indicators of the differences in how we like to learn information.

Whether we're three or ninety-three, our brains want the answers to basic questions when we learn. The Core Questions are based on a K-12 curriculum design tool known as 4MAT.[27] I learned about it in 2001 from the brilliant Jeanine Blackwell, who learned it from the equally brilliant Bernice McCarthy, Ph.D., the educator who pioneered this model.[28] Together, they recalibrated it for adult-learning and business settings. The essential curiosity built into this educational tool is perfect for helping each of us become better at giving and receiving information at work.

The Core Questions are: Why, What, How and If

Using the Core Questions is straightforward, but their simplicity can be misleading. There's power in these four questions and the biggest thing you need to remember is *how* to ask them and to answer *all* of them—not just the ones you like best.

---

27 McCarthy, Bernice Finan. *LEARNING STYLES: IDENTIFICATION AND MATCHING TEACHING FORMATS.* Northwestern University, 1979.

28 Both of these women have written about these models extensively, and if you want the deep dive about these questions from an education and training perspective, read Blackwell's book *Engage,* and McCarthy and Blackwell's *Hold On, You Lost Me!*

Every person wants to know the answers to the Core Questions but every one of us has a question we gravitate toward when we're learning something new. That's part of what makes communication challenging at work: **we assume that everyone cares about the same questions and answers we do**. That is not the case. If you look up the distribution of preference for each of the four questions—Why, What, How, and If—they tend to be pretty evenly split. This means that, if you're sharing information with a group of people, you run the risk of losing nearly 75% of the group's interest if you only focus on the question *you* like to ask or answer the most.

A key to working better with humans is acknowledging that not everyone does things the same way. We each have different styles in how we work, think, and communicate. The handy thing about people is that, while we are each different, there are common themes in how we approach learning and communication. When we get good at asking and answering the four Core Questions, we connect to the humanity in our coworkers and we get better at the communication skills that make working with them easier and more efficient. But first, you must acknowledge that everybody is different.

Framework of the Core Questions:

Why

This addresses the background of a topic and why it is relevant to the person learning the information. This question establishes the context of the topic and **why people care**. It can include the general history of the topic, the people, and the emotions involved. This question is about the **personal connection** individuals have to a topic.

> *Example: "Have you ever had to try to get a three-year-old in the middle of a tantrum into a car seat? Ever witnessed a toddler's meltdown in a restaurant? That's the type of experience we want to avoid for our customers when we launch this new version of our software. We want to ensure that they feel prepared, cared for, and have a nap before they go live."*

What

This relates the information people need to know—it's the **data and the details**. This is the checklist of the specifics of your topic that people need so they can coordinate future action. This question **shares knowledge and expertise**.

> *Example: "For this software launch to go well, we need to be organized and well-coordinated as a team. If we look at the success rate and impact scores for customer experience over the last three years, we see that detailed timelines and daily updates from us improve our customers' experience by 34%. You'll find the launch matrix in your project dashboard. Everyone is expected to read it and update their calendars by next Monday, end of day."*

How

This question is about **action**—what will people be able to do with what you are communicating? How will they **use the information** you've shared? This helps everyone **practice** what they will be expected to do and know the steps needed to do it.

> *Example: "You are responsible for knowing your role, working to the timeline, and noticing whether our plan is working or not. If you find glitches in the plan, test them out and update the project lead, and please offer a potential solution within twenty-four hours of your observation. This keeps us all in the loop and helps spot potential problems before they start. Let's get to it."*

If

This question asks about the **future** and the **vision of what will happen** if the new information being discussed is used effectively. It is about taking new information and applying it in various, often abstract circumstances. It gives people a vision of why the information you've shared is relevant to future goals and ties back into WHY the topic or action matters to them.

> *Example: "Our goal is to have this rollout go smoothly for our customers. That is always our North Star, and you now know the details of how to meet that goal. As we move forward, remember that we*

want to learn as we go, so make note of which processes work well in this launch and can be applied elsewhere. That can help everyone feel confident and supported in the future."

When you talk with your coworkers about the work that needs to be done, you may tend to focus on **What** and **How**: what to do and how to do it. Both questions are vital for accuracy and consistency, plus they help everyone get stuff done. But you need to include **Why** and **If** so you aren't alienating the work from its context, meaning, and its relevance to everyone's future.

Keep the Core Questions in mind when you have a conversation, and your communication will improve exponentially. Practice using the questions you like to skip, and you will be amazed.

You may think, "These seem simple; I feel like I already use them." You're right. You do. But *simple* is not the same as *easy*. You ask these questions every day, but you probably aren't making the most of them.

Core Questions – Worksheet

What do you want to talk about? What's your topic? Keep that in mind as you ask and answer each of the four Core Questions. A little bit of reflection to organize your ideas before a conversation can help you prepare for the unexpected and connect more effectively with others.

You can start by asking yourself any of these questions, but make sure you ask and answer all in preparation for sharing information with others. Keep asking good questions and notice how each one can support the clarity of the others.

★ It's often handiest to ask WHY first –
then you know why you care, too.

*IF everyone uses this information or skill well, what will happen? What's the **VISION** for the future? What do you hope will happen? How might this information be applied elsewhere?*

*This question gives background and **CONTEXT** to the information. It engages others with examples and experiences they can relate to and care about. WHY helps you share why the topic is relevant and important.*

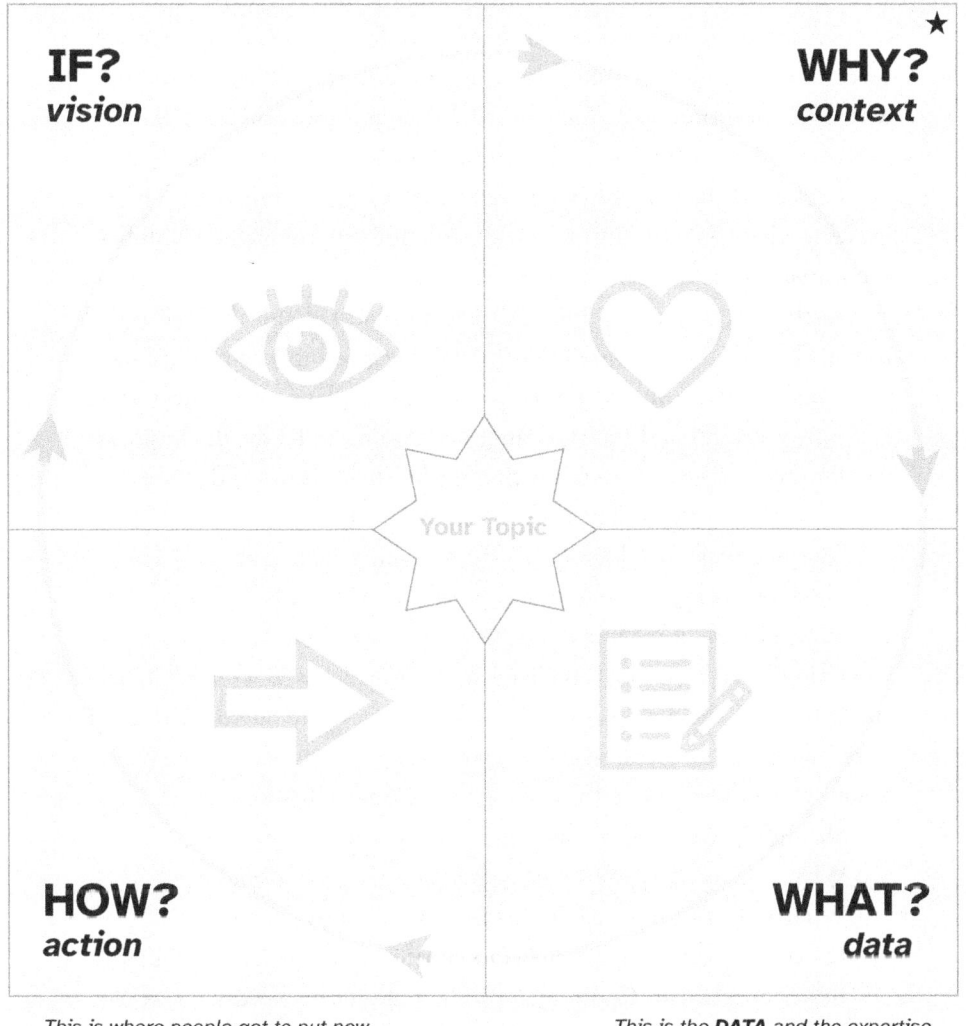

IF?
vision

WHY?
context

HOW?
action

WHAT?
data

This is where people get to put new information into **ACTION**. This is where everyone (including you) gets to practice and experiment with HOW ideas and next steps can work.

This is the **DATA** and the expertise behind it. WHAT is made of the specific list of details people need to know to be effective in using new information.

Souce: Adapted from About Learning and 4MAT4Business

A Benefit of the Core Questions

Claire owns a successful salon and day spa. She is a skilled, savvy, and deeply caring entrepreneur. Claire's enthusiasm for education about both business and personal growth is powerful, which is why I was excited to work with her when she reached out for communication help.

She was announcing a new business plan for the upcoming year but was concerned that her team wasn't buying into it, and she wasn't sure why. Her confusion was compounded by the positive working relationships among the team. They all liked each other, so what was the deal?

I attended the companywide staff meeting and within twenty minutes saw what Claire meant: the staff was polite but not aligned with her excitement. I also understood why.

At the end of the meeting, Claire was exhausted and the staff were friendly but flat. As the two of us debriefed the meeting, Claire asked me, "Do you see what I mean? I'm telling them our plans for the next year and how powerful and transforming this is going to be for the business and for their careers. I have so much hope for their futures and all we can accomplish! Why don't they see how important this is?"

"Because they don't know what the hell you're talking about, Claire."

She looked at me, shocked, and then broke into a belly laugh, "No wonder they look at me like I'm delusional—they think I am!"

Claire wasn't delusional and her team wasn't clueless. But Claire, in her enthusiasm for the new plans, got stuck in her favorite question, **If**. She talked about the next year in esoteric and abstract terms because she had a vision, and she's very skilled at making her visions profitable realities.

She didn't give her staff answers to the other three questions:

Why—the context for the new plan and why they would care
What—the details of what they needed to know
How—the actions they needed to take to bring the details to life

In her excitement, Claire forgot to include all the pieces that would have made it easy for every person to understand her vision and get excited, too.

Here are more examples of what favoring one question can look like in meetings and conversations at work:

- Too much **Why** (Context)
    - You're constantly checking to make sure everyone feels the topic is important before it's discussed—the meeting gets stuck before it gets started.
    - The history or background info about a topic drags on and on.
    - You give lots of explanation about the context but no illustration of how the information is useful to individuals. They never know what they should do with all the context or why it matters to them.
- Too much **What** (Data)
    - These meetings could have been emails because they are often just task lists and reports.
    - You over-explain and have exorbitant deference to "experts" without the inclusion of expertise that may be in the room. There is a tendency to think there is only one expert (and that person is often the authority who micromanages).
    - You belabor the minutiae that can be read or researched on one's own; you sometimes sound like you're reading aloud from a textbook.
- Too much **How** (Action)
    - You dive into the action plan without any background or detail, "Here's what has to happen. Go figure it out!"
    - You avoid or dismiss questions that ask for clarity of information and specifics.
    - You have no interest in exploring the implications of what is being done; emphasis on "building the plane as we fly it" (you may completely miss the fact that what's actually needed is a boat).
- Too much **IF** (Future-focus)
    - You present your vision for the new strategic plan with excitement, but you mention nothing about how the plan will become reality or what the next steps may be. You tend to leave the details to someone else.

- The person who is leading the conversation, which may or may not be you, seems to be jumping into a thought mid-stream.
- The meeting is about one thing at the beginning and morphs into three *different* things by the end (you may have lost your audience completely).

Examples of How to Use the Core Questions:

For yourself: When you're in a meeting, listen to whether the Core Questions are being answered—by paying attention to context, data, action, and vision. If you notice information is missing (for example, if you don't know why the company is opening a new office in icy Greenland), ask follow-up questions: "Thanks for giving us so much data on the housing opportunities for those relocating to the new Greenland office. Will you please tell us more about the background of the decision and why it's important to create an Arctic outpost on the world's largest island?" Yes, this may sound obvious but remember that's what we are learning here: how to attend to the obvious bits of communication that keep getting lost or forgotten.

When managing others: Prepare for the meeting as an individual, thinking about the information that you want to share and learn. Then focus on the type of information your team gravitates toward:

- Who springs into action before they know what they are doing or why (they are most interested in How)? Let your team know that they can focus on taking action after you discuss how the information will be applied (the What and If questions).
- Are there people on your team who want to spend time discussing the topic because they need context to feel grounded (the Why question) or want to focus only on specifics (the What question)? Give your team the information they need to be more comfortable.
- Together, you can answer all the Core Questions.

When you deliberately use the Core Questions to help you communicate well at work, you can share information confidently and people will understand the importance of what you're saying more quickly. You create a clearer picture that has a better chance of reaching the different people on your team, and you have a much better chance of creating buy-in.

You don't have to worry about using the questions perfectly—this isn't a book about the precise use of K-12 curriculum design tools. It's about quickly making use of your curiosity, clarifying your own understanding, and appreciating what someone else—another human—may want to know. It's about making your information meaningful, clear, and useful to other humans. You know, the humanity-centered stuff of communication.

Practice slowing down to consider these questions and you'll save yourself so much time and irritation. There will be less need for clean-up or explanation after the fact, and less possibility of confusion and other humans digging in their heels because they don't get it. Ask:

- **Why**—Why do they care and why may they be interested? Engage the context and show why this topic is something people care about.
- **What**—What information needs to be shared? What are the *specific* details that add clarity?
- **How**—How can they practice using this information and put it into action?
- **If**—If they begin applying this information to their work, what's the outcome and how will they feel?

With a little practice, these questions can be asked and answered quickly, and you will easily use them in real-time. *You can also dive deeper with some of the Resources and References at the back of this book.*

Four Things to Do Forever–
Let's Get Clear

Think of a time when you became frustrated, fed-up, or disappointed because someone didn't do what you expected them to. A key data point didn't make it into a slide deck, a client wasn't called when scheduled, someone didn't check for dietary restrictions and the ten vegans at your lunch event got seriously hangry while staring at a pile of turkey sandwiches. Whatever the situation, grab a piece of paper, and write down what you expected or hoped would happen. Then write down what actually happened.

Disappointing Situation

What I Expected to Happen   What Actually Happened

_____   _____

Now think about a time when a conversation or plan went well. What was the circumstance? How did you feel when you realized that everything was going smoothly? What did you say to your coworkers after things ended well? Maybe you were expecting that a colleague would disagree with your recommendation, but as you took the time to discuss the situation, you found out you both wanted the same thing. Whatever your experience, write it down.

Satisfying Situation

What I Expected to Happen   What Actually Happened

_____   _____

These contrasting experiences will be your reference point as we dive into the second communication tool to make working with humans easier: the Four Things to Do Forever.

The Four Things to Do Forever are incredibly helpful in a fantastically boring way: if you practice these four things in every conversation that involves a next step and repeat them forever—and I mean FOR-EV-ER—your communication will become clearer, more effective, more inclusive, and lend itself to better results and relationships. Those outcomes make the boring nature of this tool totally worthwhile.

The Four Things to Do Forever are:
1. Communicate Clearly
2. Establish Expectations
3. Get Commitment
4. Follow Through

1. Communicate Clearly

This is the mostly easy part.

Communicating clearly sounds obvious. In many ways, it is—know what you want to say and say it. "Shawn, please review the agenda for tomorrow's team retreat and make sure everyone has a copy." Check. Shawn has been told to do something and should do it. It's his job.

But communicating clearly, this first step, is not about Shawn. Communicating clearly is about YOU. You are the person who oversees what comes out of your mouth when you communicate. You must begin the Four Things with yourself and your awareness of the topic at hand.

To communicate clearly, start by asking yourself a few background questions.

- What is the purpose or goal of this conversation?
- Why do I care about it?
- What do I need to say?
- What do I hope will happen?
- How will I know if it works?

These questions build on your Character Compass and the Core Questions of Why, What, How, and If. When you take the time to reflect on the background and context of what you want to say, it helps build confidence in your own knowledge and why you want to say it. You become more prepared to have a conversation with others because you know the context.

Let's use the example with Shawn to illustrate possible answers to the questions above.

- What is the purpose of this conversation?
    - *We're getting closer to the event. I want to ensure that everyone is prepared and that we catch any last-minute snags before they happen.*
- Why do I care about it?
    - *I want to manage my anxiety about the details. I also want everyone to feel excited about the day. It's going to be fun.*
- What do I need to say?
    - *Check on the agenda and make sure everyone gets a copy.*
- What do I hope will happen?
    - *That Shawn does what I ask; that he looks at the agenda, reviews it thoroughly, and shares it; that everyone gets a copy or the link, and that we're all prepared and excited about the event.*
- How will I know if it works?
    - *If Shawn finds any problems, he fixes them; if we see potential snags, we prevent them; and we get this information to others and check off one more task that moves us toward a great day tomorrow.*

Conversations that are anchored in a clear, specific context are more productive and satisfying for everyone.[29] And they become even more satisfying with the second step: Establish Expectations.

---

29 That said, I'm a HUGE fan of a rambling chat. I think out loud all the time, and talking with others is often how I discover what I want to say or know. But part of communicating clearly has to do with knowing WHEN to chat and when to get clear and solid in what you want to say and why.

2. Establish Expectations

This is the occasionally awkward part. Clumsiness is okay.

Have you heard the saying, "The surest way to avoid disappointment is to let go of expectations"? There is a beauty in that statement that speaks volumes about the nature of non-attachment and that can bring mindful awareness to your life. I'm all for being attuned to the present moment, but there is a step missing: **we must identify what our expectations *are* before we can let go of them.** Also, for the sake of working better with humans, we don't want to let go of *all* expectations because they're how stuff gets done. What we need to do is make good use of our expectations. We need to understand, share, and refine them as needed. That's how we prevent disappointing ourselves and each other at work.

Disappointment grows from *unmet* expectations. But that's not the fault of expectations themselves or of the humans who hold those expectations. The problem lies in expectations that are *unspoken* and *assumed*. Tacit expectations are a recipe for disaster. We need to know what our expectations are, discuss them openly with others, discover if they are workable, agree to them, and then get to work on bringing them to life.

The Label "Expectations"

When I say "Establish Expectations," depending on your personal history and your experiences with the word *expectation*, it may sound pushy or blunt. All too often in our culture, the word expectation is about unhelpful attitudes:

- Judgmental or dismissive, as in, "Well, what did you *expect*?"
- Hyper-critical, as in, "You have failed to meet my expectations." Followed by a frown.
- Patronizing, as in, "If you can meet the expectation, then I'll know you're able to move on like a good little minion."

All those examples are reasons why we hesitate to be explicit about our expectations. We don't state them because we don't want to insult anyone.

Not insulting each other is a key part of working better with humans, and we will discuss this in the chapter on Key Behaviors. But when we don't state our expectations in hopes that people will just "get it," we allow ourselves not to think about our expectations clearly, and they fade into the background as though they are unimportant.

**Expectations are a part of life.
Knowing what they are and where they come from is vital
to communicating well with others.**

Discovering Your Own Expectations
Let's look at the example of Shawn again and identify some expectations that would be good to understand and share. In the text below, I've emphasized terms that can be loaded with unspoken expectations and tacit assumptions—the stuff that people should, like, *know*.

- What is the purpose of this conversation?
    - *We're getting closer to the event. I want to **ensure** that **everyone** is **prepared** and that we catch any last-minute snags before they happen.*

- Why do I care about it?
    - *I want to manage my anxiety about the details. I also want everyone to **feel excited** about the day. It's going to be fun.*

- What do I need to say?
    - ***Check** on the agenda and make sure everyone gets a copy.*

- What do I hope will happen?
    - *That Shawn does what I ask; that he looks at the agenda, reviews it **thoroughly**, and shares it; that everyone gets a copy or the link, and that we're all **prepared** and excited about the event.*

- How will I know if it works?
    - *If Shawn **finds any problems, he fixes** them; if we see potential snags, **we prevent them**; and we get this information to others and check off one more task that moves us toward a **great day** tomorrow.*

What do you notice about the highlighted text? They are words and concepts people often define differently. You may have a different expectation about what it means to do something "thoroughly" than Shawn does. Shawn may be working from a different list of "everyone" than you are. While words like "thoroughly," "important," and "prepared" may feel obvious, they aren't.

Here's a common example that makes lots of people a little bonkers: being *on time*.

If I ask you to be on time for an in-person meeting at 1 p.m., when will you arrive? When will your favorite colleague arrive? What about your workplace nemesis? Your girlfriend, partner, uncle, dentist? (*Why are all of these people at this meeting?*) Does the time you arrive change if you're hosting the meeting? If you are bringing the snacks? The flip chart?

Maybe, for you, on time means being at least five minutes early. Your favorite colleague may be awesome, but they define being on time as three to five minutes late. Your workplace nemesis is meticulously punctual and arrives ten minutes early to everything, so they can be focused and calm, with a pen in hand, at the exact moment the meeting is scheduled to start (*Dammit, your nemesis has a trait you kind of appreciate*).

When was the last time you discussed a definition for being on time? Think about how often we're disappointed or annoyed by the timeliness of others. Now think about how your stress level would go down if everyone had the same definition of being on time and then *used* that shared definition *to be* on time. What if it was out in the open that some people love to be early and some people get stuck in a time warp between meetings? Would it feel weird to have a conversation about being on time? Probably a little; you don't want to insult people, but you need to break the avoidance habit, be a little clumsy, and have discussions about what you expect and why. A fundamental part of getting better at working with humans is acknowledging your own surprise or frustration about the things you assume "everyone knows" and using these tools to create *shared* expectations.

The fastest way to get comfortable with expectations is by doing a quick inventory of them. Let's stick with being on time.

THE COMMUNICATION MUST-HAVES

- What does being on time mean to you and how do you define it?
- Why is that your definition? (Example: Were you raised to be punctual? Did you learn about being on time from playing a sport or being in a marching band?)
- What about it is important to you?
- Where did you learn that definition of on time?
- Is there any aspect of being on time you'd like to change?
  - *Perhaps you'd love to stop being perpetually late?*
  - *Maybe you'd love to be able to get crazy and arrive only two minutes early rather than your habitual fifteen.*

Whatever your definition, it's important that you understand where it came from and what your expectations are so that you can share them with others, set a mutually agreed-upon expectation, and use it to create interactions that are satisfying rather than disappointing.[30] Predictable rather than unexpected.

Look back at the list you made about a time when people didn't deliver on what you'd hoped. When you read over it, were there expectations that weren't met? Ask yourself if the people who didn't do what you expected knew what your expectations were. This is essential: *don't assume they did.* Be ridiculously honest with yourself. Were you relying on the psychic abilities of your team to "just know" the right way to do something? Had a similar situation been fine before, and you thought everyone would simply repeat the process? Ask yourself: did I explicitly share my expectations and hopes? Did miscommunicated expectations contribute to my disappointment?

Use the Expectations Inventory worksheets below to explore how to understand your expectations so that you can discuss them clearly with others. This is an important part of eliminating those unwanted surprise conversations.

---

30 If you are thinking, "Oh, great …I have to do this, too?! I have to do everything for everyone—down to the definition of terms like *on time*?!" Yes, and no. This section is about you and your own understanding of and responsibility for the ways you communicate. We'll talk about interpersonal responsibility and how everyone needs to have responsibility for their own behavior. This section is about building your awareness of the places where you may be unintentionally and unnecessarily tripping over your own assumptions.

Expectations Inventory

Use the chart below to think about the behavioral expectations you have at work. Very often, there are details within our expectations that we don't even know or think about until we take the time to look. Do the following:

1. List the top three behaviors you find frustrating in other people at work (frustrations can be a shortcut to identifying your expectations).
2. Write down a specific example of when you have been frustrated by that behavior.
3. Describe what you assumed or hoped would happen instead.
4. Examine what you hoped would happen. What are the underlying qualities of character that you expect to see enacted? (These are important points for future discussions.)

Read the example below then start to inventory your expectations on the page that follows.

	Frustrating Behavior	People who interrupt and talk over the ideas and input of others meetings.
	Specific Example	In our team's weekly check-ins, two senior members routinely talk over junior staff and dismiss their questions.
Behavior I Expected	What I had assumed would happen	• I expect better manners. • I expect people to be attentive to each other's contributions. • I expect a meeting facilitator to intervene.
	Underlying Expectation	• Inclusion – all people present can contribute • Structure – that there is order to meetings • Courtesy – toward all participants

THE COMMUNICATION MUST-HAVES

Expectations Inventory: Worksheet

Frustrating Behaviors	1
	2
	3

Frustrating Behavior #1	
Specific Example	
Behavior I Expected — What I had assumed would happen	
Behavior I Expected — **Underlying Expectation**	

Frustrating Behavior #2	
Specific Example	
Behavior I Expected — What I had assumed would happen	
Behavior I Expected — **Underlying Expectation**	

Frustrating Behavior #3	
Specific Example	
Behavior I Expected — What I had assumed would happen	
Behavior I Expected — **Underlying Expectation**	

Now, look at the expectations you identified on the previous page. In the space below, pick one and explore how you came to expect this behaviors in the workplace. Then start to examine why these are important to you and whether others know about and can meet this expectation*. Examining your expectations is an essential part of being able to communicate well.

Underlying Expectation	*Courtesy*
When did I learn it and from whom?	*I learned it from my granddad when I was a little kid.*
Why is it important to me?	*I know it's useful to build and maintain relationships at work; I like knowing I'm using what I learned from my granddad.*
Do other people know I have this expectation?	*Yes (they know, right...? doesn't everyone expect this?)*
Have I talked directly about this expectation?	*I think so, but the conversation could be clarified.*

Underlying Expectation	
When did I learn it and from whom?	
Why is it important to me?	
Do other people know I have this expectation?	
Have I talked directly about this expectation?	

* ***A note about expectations:*** "High standards" can be good, but if your standards are never met, it can be a signal to explore the expectations that created those standards. Examining who always or never meets your expectations can be a good place to start uncovering implicit cultural biases.

THE COMMUNICATION MUST-HAVES

You may be asking, "How in the name of all that's holy am I supposed to bring up my expectations with others without sounding like a dork? I can't tell people I want to talk about being *on time*. That's weird."

What if it's only weird because we're not used to doing it? Imagine a scenario with you and all of the people I mentioned above (your colleagues, your boss, your partner, your uncle, your dentist). I'm facilitating a meeting for you. To begin, I say:

"I'm looking forward to working with you. One of the things that will help this work go well is having shared expectations about how we want to work together. Unclear expectations can lead to miscommunication and frustration, and while it may seem obvious that people rarely intend to do bad work or miscommunicate, let's start with something that each of us usually has a slightly different definition of: what does it mean to be 'on time'?"

Then we'd have a conversation and, if nothing else, we'd understand what the differences were in the room. We'd know who defines being on time as being ten minutes early and who has a very loose relationship to the time-space continuum.

Would that feel weird? Maybe, but when we practice (remember: you are going to do these four things *for-ev-er*), it can begin to feel normal. It can feel like a huge relief.

When we have conversations about our expectations, they become easier. We can all be on the same page—quite literally, if you write everyone's expectations down in one shared spot.

When you use the Expectations Inventory, you have another tool to work better with other humans, prevent surprises and disappointments, and troubleshoot potential miscommunication before it happens. That doesn't mean that you won't ever be disappointed in your team or yourself; it means that you will be more confident in your conversations as you get into the meaty part of the Four Things to Do Forever: Get Commitment.

3. Get Commitment

This is where the action is. Are you ready?

How many times have you asked someone to do something and they don't quite follow through? They delay, forget, or even do the opposite of what you were hoping for. It might have been something as simple as a coworker not having prepared a meeting's agenda as they said they would. Or you'd thought that your co-presenter was bringing all of the day's materials and then discovered that they only remembered they'd agreed to it ninety minutes before the program was supposed to begin (I only made that mistake once).

Whatever the circumstance, there are three central reasons people don't do things the way you want them:
1. You don't ask (you prefer to rely on the Psychic Employee Network for all your communication needs).
2. You aren't clear about your expectations when you do ask (see previous section on expectations).
3. You assume the other humans you work with have made a commitment to do the work but no human has said, "Yes, I will do that," or "No, I will not," or anything about what they are agreeing to do or not do.

You are probably doing all of these things more frequently than you realize.

Getting a commitment from another human about an action requires them to say, "Yes, I will do that" or "No, I will not" or "I will do this but not that." In other words, clarity of agreement. It is more specific than an acknowledgment of information. For another person to say "Yes, I will do that," or "No, I won't," you need to ask, "Will you do this?" It is a yes or no question and is vital to communicating well with other people at work. It can feel uncomfortable because asking for a commitment is a direct, sometimes bold, thing to do. Because it is missing in so many of our communications, we have unexpected and surprising conversations.

Asking for a specific response, *yes* or *no*, is so simple it can seem reductive, like you're talking down to your colleague, even being rude. Your manner and attitude when you ask close-ended (yes/no) questions matters, as we will see in the chapter about Key Behaviors, and that is why you have your Character Compass and the Core Questions in hand. When you ask for a commitment to action, it is important that you know the background and why you are asking. Being clear makes direct communication easier. It feels better, too.

Asking for commitment for simple things like sending an email or picking up lunch may feel like overdoing it. Do you have to be so specific on simple things? Isn't that kind of intense? Isn't it micro-managing? If you're asking in a super-intense way: "Brian! I beseech you to deliver this letter to the mailroom by 3 p.m.! Will you give me your commitment that you shall do so?!" Yes, that may be a little much. Brian may worry that you are going to ask him to swear fealty to the Marketing Department with a blood oath and pledge of his firstborn child. That would *definitely* be overdoing it.

But saying, "Brian, this letter needs to be in the mailroom before 3 p.m.; will you please make sure it's delivered?" and waiting for Brian to say, "Yes, I sure will," then responding, "Thank you"—that's completely reasonable.

What if Brian affably responds to your request with, "On it" or "Put it on the pile of stuff on my desk" or a sincere and humorous, "You know how I love running to the mailroom"? Might you take those as a *yes*? Maybe. Just know that none of those answers *is* a *yes*.

Why does it matter? *It matters because good communication at work involves building a history of clear, deliberate confidence in one another.* Direct commitment to the seemingly little things like delivering the mail is what creates reliability and trust over time. If you ask for commitment about little things like mail, it makes asking for commitment on deadlines, working with challenging customers, or sharing potential pitfalls easier—more of a delight and less of a drag.

But how do you get a *yes* if you've been told, "Put it on the pile of stuff on my desk"? Isn't that awkward? Only if you make it awkward, and only if you're not clear on Why you're asking and What your expectations are—the first two of the Four Things to Do Forever and the Core Questions.

If you hear something that sounds like *yes* but isn't quite, check. "So, yes, you will take it to the mailroom by 3 p.m.?" Brian will say *yes*. Most people will reiterate what they meant with their vague response when you are sincerely looking for clarity.

But Brian may hear you more clearly when you ask again for specific commitment. He may hear you, register what you have said differently, and then he may say *no*. *No is a perfectly fine response!* It's fine because then there is an opportunity for conversation and discovery. You must be comfortable with hearing *no* to discover a path to a shared *yes*.[31]

This can feel jarring because many of us were taught that saying *no* to our boss is rude or could be a quick way to get fired. If Brian says *no* to

---

31 Please note that finding commitment and finding a way to a *yes* answer in work-related actions is different from the yes/no conversations around consent and physical intimacy. There is linguistic and contextual overlap, but the two arenas are different. Please reference the Resources section for more information.

a trip to the mailroom, your knee-jerk reaction to Brian may be, "Dude, suck it up and make it happen." But, for this exercise, and in general, resist that urge. Instead, ask, "Why?"

Brian may tell you that he said *no* because the mailroom is closed today due to a water leak in the basement but that he will make sure the envelope gets to the post office before it closes and asks if that would be okay. Brian may tell you he's on his way to the dentist for a root canal but that Monique is covering his mail run this afternoon, and she's picking up everything off his desk at 2:45 p.m. Brian may confess that he has been meaning to talk to you about his secret phobia of the basement mailroom and has been wondering how to tell you about it, so he said to put it on his desk to avoid the conversation.

Whatever the reason, if you ask for commitment and the answer is *no*, then you can discover if a commitment is still on the table under different circumstances. This doesn't mean that you must negotiate, but it means that Brian may need to commit to finding an alternative solution and ensuring that the job gets done, mailroom phobia or not. From your perspective, this conversation may sound like, "Okay. We can talk about the mailroom in a broader sense tomorrow in our weekly meeting. Right now, will you find a way to ensure that the mail gets to the mailroom by 3 p.m.?"

"Yes, I will."

"Thanks, Brian."

All of this is a conversation, which is where the action is when you work with humans. Without a conversation about commitment, actions become vague: "You wanted that out today? I'll try to get to it tomorrow." You can feel the disappointment and frustration seeping in and dragging you down, can't you?

Yes or *no*. When the communication is clear and the expectations are set, either is fine. Because then you know who is committed to doing what, and you can build confidence in how you work with and manage others.

You may think getting commitment to something like a run to the mailroom is too simple. But it's not. It lets you practice. When you practice with the seemingly easy stuff, it makes the trickier stuff easier to spot and handle.

Take, for example, my dear friend and colleague Nicole.[32]

It's Not a Yes

When I work with leadership teams and executive coaching clients, part of what I do is help managers improve their own coaching skills so their teams are successful. It can be pretty specific work, and good listening is required on everyone's part. Nicole came to me for help managing her sales staff. Each member of her team was competent and easy to work with, good eggs all around. Therefore, when Sam, the most experienced and friendly of the bunch, kept failing to close contracts on time, Nicole was concerned. She talked with him, reminded him of the importance of deadlines, and emphasized that closing sales was how the firm made money. She told him that his work was important. Sam would then apologize for his failures and pledge to do better next time.

The situation was becoming fraught. Sam was avoidant of conversations with coworkers, and his work was suffering. Nicole started to document every sales conversation so she knew that the expectations were clear: date, scope of work, price, signatures needed, etc. She knew that Sam meant to do better, but by the third corrective conversation, she was so frustrated he wasn't getting the job done that she was ready to toss him

---

[32] This is her actual name!

out on his ear. She called me to discuss disciplinary action and potential termination.

To double-check the situation, I asked, "Have you communicated clearly? Does he understand what you're discussing?"

She said, "Yes! It's in writing and we've gone over it repeatedly, for months now."

"Are the expectations clear? Have you been explicit as to what he is to do?"

"Yes. I told him that if he didn't close and finish his paperwork as specified that he was going to be fired."

"Did you ask him to commit to meeting the expectations?"

"Yes! That's why it's so confusing."

"And what exactly did he say when you asked if he would meet the expectation?"

"He looked at me then hung his head, he was so embarrassed, and said, 'Nicole, I hear you loud and clear.'"

I paused before I asked, "He said what?"

"He said, 'Nicole, I hear you loud and clear.'"

"What part of 'I hear you loud and clear' means, 'Yes, I will do that'?"

"Shit."

"Exactly. He didn't commit."

Sam wasn't trying to be a jerk, he just didn't know how to express that closing a sale was becoming something he dreaded. Despite his years of experience, he'd lost his interest in sales and thought he could fake his way through it. By never officially saying *yes* or *no*, he was trying to give himself an out. He *did* hear Nicole and *did* understand why it was important, but then he got stuck in a vicious cycle of avoidance that sabotaged his results.

Nicole talked to him about her expectations again, this time saying that she was looking for *yes* or *no*. Their conversation opened up from there. It turned out that Sam hated closing sales so much that he was looking for a different job. But he loved her company and being of help to other members of the team, so he was trying to make it work. Nicole told him that his work mattered but that she didn't want either of them to struggle. They created a new expectation about how to have him exit gracefully without him getting fired or Nicole having to scramble to find someone to replace him on short notice.

When you ask for an answer that is either *yes* or *no*, listen to the response. *Yes* is great, but *no* is okay, too. *No*, in daily conversations, can yield, "Why not? Say more." *No*s can build better clarity and cultivate responsibility and solutions that you didn't know were there. The job can still get done.

And once you hear *yes*, you're ready for the fourth thing to do forever: Follow Through.

4. Follow Through

This is where you close the loop, and everyone knows what's up.

You've Communicated Clearly, Established Expectations, and Gotten Commitment—well done! Let's bring your skills home and work on the last of the four things: Follow Through.

This step is elegant and intentional. It's also wonderful because it's not all on you. This step is shared between you and the person you're communicating with.

Once you Get Commitment, you establish a check-in point with the person who has committed to the expectation. It's a way to close the loop and complete things with confidence and ease. All you do is make note of the agreed-upon deadlines or commitments, then follow through to check on progress. Responsibility doesn't have to rest solely with you—the person making the commitment can be responsible for checking in. It's like having someone else help you with your to-do list.

Let's go back to Brian. When he says *yes*, he's going to handle the mail, you may reply, "Thanks. Will you let me know when it's posted? I'll feel better knowing that it's on its way." Brian, because he's a responsive human and hears that you are clearly communicating your need for follow-through, will say *yes*.

Because he's not a schmuck, he will follow through when he's done and say, "I mailed the letter. You can breathe easy." It was his responsibility to follow through and he did. The loop is closed, and the task is done.

If Brian committed to mailing the letter and to following through and did not close the loop with you, you can ask him if it was posted. He may have forgotten to let you know it was mailed or may have forgotten to mail it altogether. Either way, *all you had to do was ask* about the committed-to action—not let it go, hoping it had happened or fuming because he didn't tell you or nervous that you should have asked someone else. If he forgot, then you make a new plan and have a new conversation.

That conversation can begin with a reference to what he committed to, "You committed to mailing the letter by 3 p.m. What happened?" You'll have a conversation about what to do next but you're starting that conversation from a place of shared information—the baseline was the commitment and the clear communication and expectations involved.

The focus of the conversation is about a specific event, not overarching blame and humans acting poorly: "Ugh, Brian is always unreliable! I can't believe I asked him to do this! He's the worst." Brian may be the worst, but you won't know that until you have clear expectations and commitments on which to base your opinion. Follow-through allows you to examine actions and commitments one at a time rather than bundling them all into a messy heap. It lets people attend to one action and one deadline at a time and course correct if needed.

You may be thinking, "Isn't this really micromanage-y?" No. Not when done well. Which you will be able to do. With practice.

Whether you are communicating with a colleague or managing a team, the intent is to be clear, swift, and deliberate when you communicate—all while avoiding unnecessary disappointment and surprise. It also doesn't have to happen every time you put something in the mail. You can apply this approach to large projects and events with lots of granular tasks that not everyone needs to hear about every day. If you are managing a project, what may be most important for you to know is who is responsible for which details, not the daily specific details themselves (number of emails sent, how many tasks remain on the twelve-month timeline, or the change in the drag coefficient on the labeling machine).

With larger projects, the key is for you to communicate what your expectations are about details, planning, and quality. Then you can get commitments from all necessary parties and follow through from there. For example, if a team has committed to completing a project on-budget, with excellent quality and superior customer service, and they deliver only two of those three things, then you can follow through on each of those specific pieces based on established expectations and commitments.

This whole process is about building a flow of communication around expectations and commitments with other humans at work. It helps people gain confidence in their understanding of what needs to be done, of how to speak up when they have practical questions—and enables them to build a sense of reliability with their coworkers.

Recap of The Four Things to Do Forever:

1. **Communicate Clearly**
   - This is all about YOU and your own clarity about the topic at hand.

2. **Establish Expectations**
   - This one can seem a little harder because sharing your expectations can feel weird.
   - Hopes and vision prime the pump for clear action and follow-through.

3. **Get Commitment**
   - This is where the action is.
   - It is a yes or no question.
   - *No* is okay. Be curious about why someone's answer is *no*. From there, you can find a solution and arrive at a commitment.

4. **Follow Through**
   - This is where everything comes together and you close the loop.
   - It's about having a point of reference when things go south or get unclear.

Four Things to Do Forever: Worksheet

For Clearer, More Effective Communication

Topic:

1. Communicate Clearly	Ask yourself: Why is this conversation important? What do I hope will be the result?
2. Establish Expectations	Ask yourself: What do I expect? Are these shared expectations? How do I know they are shared? Do I know the other person's expectations? Clarifying expectations is vital to success.
3. Get Commitment	This is a perfect place for a close-ended question! If the answer is no, stay curious and discover Why. Refine and discover what will work until everyone says yes. (Beware of answers like, "I get it" or "I hear you loud and clear." Those are positive statements that are not necessarily, "YES.")
4. Follow Through	DO NOT FORGET THIS STEP. It's where trust and confidence are built.

Becoming a better, more resilient communicator is like becoming better at anything. It requires learning the essential components of the task and practicing each of them—forever.

Consistently practicing each of the four things will improve your skills as a communicator. This process will help you clarify your thoughts, articulate your expectations, build cooperative dialogue, and increase your confidence in communicating with others.

The steps are simple. Simple does not mean easy. Practice, practice, practice.

Unexpected Conversations:
Communication Must-Haves

One of the spots where people have a hard time with communication is when they don't know the answer to a question:

- "Why does our company have this policy around sick leave?"
- "What should I say when I tell her we're behind schedule?"
- "How do you expect me to get that done on time?"
- "If we do that, what will happen to the customers we're already committed to?"

And the big one:

- "Why do we do it *this* way?"

Whether you manage only yourself or yourself and many others, here's the secret to facing any of those types of questions: you *don't* have to know all the answers. You *do* have to be willing to ask and learn about what you don't know.

The greatest misconception that people in any role and any level of experience have is that they think they are supposed to have perfect answers to every question. If you're in a new role, you probably hoped that all those answers would download magically to your brain when your business cards arrived.

There is no magical download, but there is one magical way of learning the answers to people's questions: be curious and go find out. How do you do that? ASK.

When you are building your skills as a communicator, remember that asking about what you don't know (and questioning what you *do* know, from time to time) is a great way to model learning for the people around you.

Imagine what could happen if, when you are asked a question you don't know the answer to (such as, "Why do we do it this way?"), you respond with, "I have an idea why we do it that way, but let me find out a few more details and get back to you." If you do some research and get back to the person, knowing that you are more confident in your knowledge, how will you feel? How may the other person feel? What if you don't have to wing it?

Think about a conversation you were surprised by, one where you felt like you had to have the answer immediately. What might have been different if you had paused, shared what you did know, said you wanted to learn more, and then followed through with that new info? Or, if pausing to learn wouldn't have been practical, what would have changed had you answered the Core Questions of Why, What, How, and If for the person who asked the surprising question? I am constantly shocked by how much my own confidence goes up when I give myself a moment or two to think about the Core Questions before I launch into answer-mode.

The cool thing about communication that is grounded in curiosity and clarity is that it promotes learning. When it's okay not to know but expected that you will ask for help and learn, then communication also promotes *shame-free* learning. And that is a great way to make working with humans a whole lot better.

Practice With a Pal:
Communication Must-Haves

What are the questions you hope no one asks you at your work? Is there a topic you think everyone else knows well but you don't understand? What about things like the history of how your organization was founded or the reason behind that change in health insurance carrier? We all have things that we're supposed to know because they are part of our job, but time-pressure and the sheer volume of stuff we have to know can make deep knowledge of all the details difficult.

Complete the following (and have your pal do the same):

- At work, these are the topics I fake my way through when asked:
    - _____
    - _____
    - _____
    - _____

- These are the topics I talk around or only give surface-level answers to because I don't feel like an expert:
    - _____
    - _____
    - _____
    - _____

- I admire _____'s knowledge about _____ that I listed above. One thing I would like to learn from them is _____.

After you fill out the lists above, pick one topic you'd like to feel more confident in and learn a bit about it. Then use the Core Questions to describe:
- **Why** you care about this. Share the context or larger background.
- **What** the details are and who you would ask for further information and data.

- **How** you will practice using this information and what you will do with it.
- **If** you learn about this topic you will feel _____.

Then apply the **Four Things to Do Forever**. You can use the same topic you've reflected on above or pick a topic or task that needs to be discussed within your team. For practice, draft answers to the following, and then test them out in an additional conversation with your pal.

1. Communicate Clearly
   State the subject and why it is important (this builds off the Core Questions).

2. Establish Expectations
   Do not make assumptions. "The expectation about this is _____."

3. Get Commitment
   "Will you do it?" is a yes/no question

4. Follow Through
   Put it on the calendar and find out if it's done.

Meet with your pal and share your lists, what you discovered about your topic, how you'd communicate the new information, and which points feel solid or shaky. All of this takes a little deliberate practice. Go forth and be curious and clear!

What's in It for YOU
and how do you know if it's working?

Checking for Communication and Adjusting as Needed

Curiosity and clarity are the cornerstones of communication and working better with humans. You need to be deliberate in how you practice both. The Core Questions and the Four Things to Do Forever build good conversations and create consistency and trust in how you share information and learn. As you practice, remember to pause when you are stuck, frustrated, or confused about some aspect of communication.[33] Then ask one of these questions: why is this important, what do I know or feel, is there a specific action I can take, and what am I looking for up ahead? Any of those questions can help you reconnect to what you want to communicate.

Things to look for as you practice the Communication Must-Haves of the Core Questions and the Four Things to Do Forever:

Signs Communication Is Working:	Signs Communication Needs Help:
Questions from others about your topic are richer and more generative.	Questions from others seem ridiculous. *Why don't they know this?!*
Coworkers are more informed about tasks and you feel confident in your own knowledge and learning.	Uncertainty and overthinking dominate and make you want to pull your hair out. *Why don't they get this?* or *Why can't I get this?*
Conversations are purposeful and relaxed because expectations are clear. Open discussion is the norm because commitment is sought and appreciated.	Rules and policies are the focus of conversations, i.e., *We are doing this because that is the policy.* Full stop.
Communication, even about weighty topics, feels lighter.	Every conversation feels like a struggle.
Miscommunication decreases and when it happens, snafus resolve more easily.	Second-guessing is commonplace and explaining what you meant takes a lot of time and energy.
Your confidence increases.	Your defensiveness is high.

---

33 Remember that when you pause—and breathe—you give yourself an extra moment in time.

The Point

99% of problems with humans at work start with a snag in communication. When you become more skilled at using good communication tools with others, your problems decrease dramatically. This is part of the unsexy yet wildly effective effort of improving your workplace.

Many of us are so habituated to the idea that our colleagues will be difficult and that there will be crazy drama and miscommunication at every turn, we forget that we can do something to change it. It won't happen overnight, but if we don't work at it, it won't change at all. The vexation of poor communication is a worn-out habit. It's interesting and even revolutionary to do something that makes things easier, more satisfying, and more generously effective. Getting good at communication accomplishes all three. It fights the dominant productivity paradigm. Think of how much energy and time you would have for yourself if your conversations and interactions at work were useful, easy, and clear. What would you be able to do with all that freed-up potential? Good communication makes breathing room in *your* life for *you*. What a priceless and delightful benefit of learning to work better with humans and infusing humanity into your workplace.

Time and Energy
(plus a quick calculation)

As you've been reading, you've probably noticed that these exercises take some effort to do. You may be thinking, "I'm supposed to do this for every conversation? I don't have time for that!" Consider the following:

1. Think about a conversation you've been avoiding at work. How long have you been putting it off? How many days or weeks have you been saying you'll get to it? If you were going to guess, how many hours have you spent *not* having a conversation or, worse, having to clean up the mess of a conversation that went poorly because it lacked clarity from the start?

2. Look at the number of hours you've spent and ask yourself,

    - "How would I have preferred to use that time? How would I feel if I wasn't avoiding or cleaning up conversations?" Write down your answers.
    - If you like to think about things from an economic perspective, do this quick calculation:

    (number of hours spent avoiding the conversation at work) x (hourly rate) = financial cost of avoidance.

    If you're salaried and working full-time, take your annual income and divide by 2,080 to calculate your hourly rate.
    (40 hours per week x 52 weeks per year)

3. Once you get good at using your Character Compass, the Core Questions, and the Four Things to Do Forever, preparation for most conversations will take less than ten minutes. When you choose to make the time to become centered and clear, you can have a more satisfying and effective conversation. Then you can use your energy more enjoyably and feel better about working with humans.

Ideas to Clarify

Notes and Reflections

HAV... "brighter horizons"

...INGS TO DO FOREVER

hills of collaboration

WE EXPECT THESE BEHA...
DON'T FORGET TO TAL...
AND SHARE THEM.

EXPECTATIONS WOR...
WHEN DISCUSSED D...

...UNICATE EARLY

THESE ALLOW YOU TO BE CLEAR

...SET ...PECTATIONS

REMEMBER PERSONAL REFLECTION

THE BEHAVIORS WITH WHICH YOU WORK, COMMUNICATE & MANAGE

3. GET ...OMMITMENT

KEY BEHAVIORS

4. FOLLOW THROUGH

BEHAVIORS ARE NEEDED TO MAKE OTHER TOOLS WORK BEST

① MANNERS & KINDNESS
② BE OF HELP
③ PRIDE IN YOUR WORK
④ DON'T BE A JACKASS

...TICE ...A ...AL

EXPECTATIONS INVENTORY

THESE INFLUENCE EVERY CHOICE & ACTION AND ARE INFORMED BY YOUR CHARACTER

coast of hard truths

The Key Behaviors

Character and Communication come in very handy as we work with the third of the Essential Tools: the Key Behaviors. The tricky part is that, without the Key Behaviors, getting good at Character and Communication is harder than it needs to be. Each tool builds off the other—both a chicken-and-egg situation and a Möbius strip of helpful reinforcement. Whenever you work with these tools, know that you will need each of them to make the others work best. It may feel strange at first, but I promise it will become second nature.

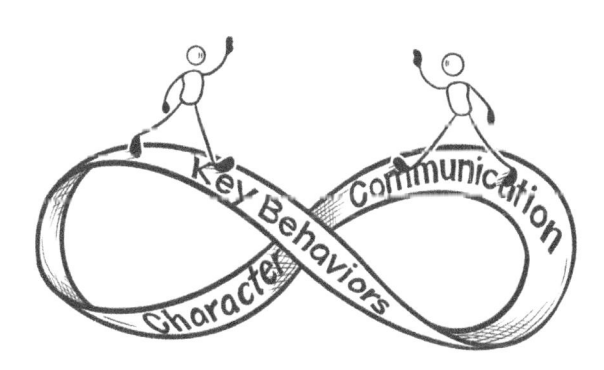

Essential Tool #3: The Key Behaviors

Have you ever worked hard on a presentation or a vacation itinerary or a family holiday meal, only to find you overlooked a vital part of the plan? Maybe you didn't proof slides with the word *public* on them for missing *L*s, or you overlooked the expiration date on your passport, or you underestimated the time it takes to thaw a turkey.

We all miss important steps in our well-intentioned plans from time to time. As you embark on this last chapter of tools that will make working with humans easier, now is *not* the time to lose focus. You've come too far! You have your Character Compass, the Core Questions, the Four Things to Do Forever, and you're ready to uncover the threads that tie them all together: the Key Behaviors. Exciting, right?

The Key Behaviors are the fundamental actions and attitudes that we expect of each other at work. They consist of three things we expect people to *do* and one thing we expect people to *avoid* at all costs. We are generally taught these things when we are young by our families, our religious communities, in early education, or in a social setting like daycare, team sports, or other group activities. Without these behaviors, children have a hard time learning the social mores that help us get along with others. As kids, we learn these behaviors early because they help create tolerance, care, and productive cooperation in any setting: they make group dynamics—and, later, work dynamics—easier.

You'd think if something was this helpful to kids at an early age, we'd keep using it throughout our lives, right? Nope. Talking about expected behaviors and attitudes on purpose? That's for kids! How patronizing and demeaning!

Sure, if you talk about these behaviors with a thirty-, sixty-, or ninety-year-old as though they haven't ever heard of them before and don't understand their importance, that *would* be insulting. But the fundamental skills we teach our kids about working cooperatively are the same behaviors we need from each other at work and in society at large. Why do we stop talking about these behaviors? Ego? Snobbery? Forgetfulness? Distraction? Misplaced optimism? Yes, all of those, and more.

Let's set the Why of it aside for a moment and reconnect to the fundamental behaviors of how to work well together. The Key Behaviors connect you with other humans in ways that honor their intelligence while effectively engaging with the situation at hand.

The Key Behaviors

1. **Share Manners and Kindness**
2. **Be of Help**
3. **Have Pride in Your Work**
4. **Don't Be a Jackass**

These four Key Behaviors are vital to making working with humans easier and better. Why? They are the unspoken expectations that we take for granted and don't know how to talk about until they are messed with—kind of like oxygen: we need it to breathe and don't notice it unless it's a little thin.

But why are these the four behaviors that make up the special sauce for better workplace communication? *Because they are what we want to experience from one another but never contextualize.* These behaviors are spoken about *obliquely* when they should be discussed *directly*. Let's look at a list of attributes and assets that employers say they want in any job posting.

Employers seek candidates who are:

- Assertive
- Thorough
- Friendly
- Prompt and responsive
- Dynamic
- Open to a flexible work schedule
- Attentive to details
- Able to own and resolve problems
- Reliable
- Service-minded
- Self-directed
- Results-oriented
- Team players
- Mature
- Credible
- Excellent communicators

Reasonable, right? Now, let's look closer to notice themes in how each of those terms may be defined. As we notice the themes in what employers are looking for when they post a job, we can learn a lot about the behavioral expectations baked into the culture that may not be openly discussed. We see the surface of the expectation, but the root of it is deeper and much more useful.

The behaviors and dispositions employers want can be categorized into at least one if not all of the following three categories: Manners and Kindness, Be of Help, and Pride in Your Work.

Manners and Kindness	Be of Help	Pride in Your Work
Assertive	*Assertive*	**Assertive**
Thorough	Thorough	**Thorough**
Friendly	Friendly	*Friendly*
Prompt and responsive	**Prompt and responsive**	Prompt and responsive
Dynamic	*Dynamic*	*Dynamic*
Open to a flexible work schedule	**Open to a flexible work schedule**	*Open to a flexible work schedule*
Attentive to details	Attentive to details	**Attentive to details**
Able to own and resolve problems	**Able to own and resolve problems**	Able to own and resolve problems
Reliable	**Reliable**	**Reliable**
Service-minded	**Service-minded**	*Service-minded*
Self-directed	Self-directed	**Self-directed**
Results-oriented	Results-oriented	**Results-oriented**
Team player	**Team player**	Team player
Mature	**Mature**	**Mature**
Credible	**Credible**	**Credible**
Excellent communicator	Excellent communicator	**Excellent communicator**

Level of daily emphasis: **High** • Medium • *Low*

When these behaviors are present, work goes more smoothly and stress decreases. When they are absent, work can feel horrible.

A Vital Note About Cynicism

> "They say that if you scratch a cynic,
> you'll find a disappointed idealist."
> —George Carlin

The single biggest drain on organizations is the time and energy wasted because people treat each other poorly. This shows up as corruption, grift, insider trading, sexual harassment, racial and religious discrimination, unequal pay, and basic rudeness from colleagues in daily interactions: taking the last of the coffee without making a new pot, parking in a spot reserved for colleagues with mobility issues, or ignoring a coworker when they say *good morning* because you're not on the clock yet. Harmful behavior is abundant in workplaces everywhere. You may be thinking of other examples and feeling your blood pressure rise. Left unchecked, bad behavior kills your spirit, your drive, and the overall health of your environment.

When you work with competent and kind people who can communicate clearly, working is easier. This is true even if the work is hard or the business is struggling. When you work with unkind or even mean people, it can be soul-crushing. You lose interest in your work and wonder why you should bother to learn to communicate better or to innovate. If the environment is too emotionally and psychologically detrimental,[34] it becomes very difficult simply to do your job. The enriching experiences you hoped for become

---

[34] Nembhard, Ingrid Marie, and A. Edmondson, "Making It Safe: The Effects of Leader Inclusiveness and Professional Status on Psychological Safety and Improvement Efforts in Health Care Teams." Special Issue on Healthcare: The problems are organizational not clinical. Journal of Organizational Behavior 27, no. 7 (November 2006): 941–966; and Edmondson, Amy C., Monica Higgins, Sara J. Singer, and Jennie Weiner. "Understanding Psychological Safety in Healthcare and Education Organizations: A Comparative Perspective." Special Issue on the Role of Psychological Safety in Human Development. Research in Human Development 13, no. 1 (2016): 65–83.

disappointments. Too much disappointment is bad for you and everyone at work and, worst of all, it breeds cynicism.

Cynicism can be the kiss of death to organizations.[35] If you currently work in a cynical culture, the road ahead is difficult. Think of the Peter Drucker quote, "Culture eats strategy for breakfast." Your company can have the best plans in the world, but if your culture is filled with the cynicism born of chronic disappointment and jackassery, those plans will never happen. Cynicism inhibits the manifestation of potential.

Cynicism isn't born of one or two negative incidents. Cynicism takes time. It takes repeated disappointments and tolerated offenses. Cynics are *disappointed idealists*—the people who once had hope. They kept having faith that things would be okay. They have ideals and know deeply that there is a better way for things to get done and for people to interact. But they can only keep popping back up for so long if the system that dismisses their spirit—their humanity—continually fails them. Eventually, it's too much to bear.

One of the most challenging aspects of repairing cynicism is that cynicism is born of deep sadness—not something we often discuss in the business world—and deep sadness can do a couple of powerful and painful things. It can cause people to give up and detach from their work. Why bother with effort if you know your work doesn't really matter? It can also make people angry. Angry that their ideas and hopes, their energies and efforts, are being wasted—and angry that they feel so powerless. Anger is potent and can be motivating but, in organizations, anger often manifests as poor behavior and jackassery, and thus the cycle

---

[35] Cynicism is not to be confused with sarcasm, though the two often go hand-in-hand. When there is too much sarcasm in a system, cynicism is often just under the surface. *Webster's Dictionary* defines *cynicism* as "the quality of one who has a cynical (adjective) attitude: a) contemptuously distrustful of human nature and motives or b) based on or reflecting a belief that human conduct is motivated primarily by self-interest." And *sarcasm* (noun) as: "a mode of satirical wit depending for its effect on bitter, caustic, and often ironic language that is usually directed against an individual."

continues. Poor behavior leads to disappointment leads to cynicism leads to poor behavior leads to ...

Then we become numb. Cynicism and poor behavior are so commonplace at work that numbness is normal. We become desensitized to bad behavior as a form of survival. But we don't have to. We don't have to feel like we're going to hell in a handbasket without a steering wheel or a handbrake. We can do something about the disappointments that lead to cynicism, and we must start by being grounded in our character and getting clear about our expectations. We must start by uncovering what we want and defining what we don't.

1. Share Manners and Kindness

> "Be kind, for everyone you meet is fighting a hard battle."
> —Plato, Philo of Alexandria, Ian MacLaren, or John Watson (depending on your source)

When you hear someone talk about having *good manners*, what comes to mind? Do you think about which fork you should use at a formal dinner table? Chewing with your mouth closed? Saying *please* and *thank you*? Holding a door for someone? Those are solid examples, but it's your awareness of their importance in your day-to-day interactions that make the difference.

Manners are important because they help us navigate interactions with other people.

Think of manners like traffic signals. If you're driving a car, understanding the rules of the road—like when to stop, how to turn, and what speed to go—is important for safety and efficiency when multiple drivers are on the road. Good manners do the same thing. Aside from the fact that saying *please* and *thank you* will help you avoid being scowled at by colleagues, there's something else that manners do—they can make you feel great when you use them.

When you have a positive interaction with other humans and feel good about it, your brain releases all sorts of excellent neuropeptides, including serotonin and oxytocin for good feelings and an uplifted mood, into your bloodstream.[36] Think about how a friend's mood lifts when you send them a kind text out of the blue, and how good you feel, too. Holding a door, smiling at the cashier in the grocery, saying *please* and *thank you* when passing food at a meal, these are all ways that we can feel better—not only because it's the polite thing to do, but because our neurochemistry helps us feel good when we do those things. Using beneficial manners makes us feel uplifted and is a convenient way we can actually help each other feel better every day.

Here are some basic manners that help make working with humans easier:

- Introduce yourself by acknowledging the other person with polite eye contact and a genuine smile. Ask the person's name and use it as you say *hello* and share your own name. "Hi, Ramon. I'm Laura. Glad to meet you." This level of explanation may seem like overkill. It's not. You will make a good impression. The more casual, "Hey, dude" is not always a winner with a new colleague or boss.
- Learn how to shake hands well.[37] Avoid the claw, being too handsy, the ghost-shake, and the dead fish.

---

[36] Pert, Candace. Molecules Of Emotion: Why You Feel the Way You Feel. United Kingdom: Simon & Schuster UK, 2012.

[37] When handshaking is not a good idea—i.e., cold, flu, and pandemic season—a kind and respectful nod/bow of the head is a fine greeting.

- Acknowledge a person by looking at them when they are speaking to you. Pay attention and acknowledge the world and humans around you.[38]
- Be patient and wait to contribute to a conversation until you are aware of the topic (e.g., the economy and Brazilian *taxes* versus a spa visit and Brazilian *waxes*.) Asking about the topic is an easy way to do this.
- Greet people kindly and directly. Smile and say hello. You make every interaction better by sharing kindness with other humans.
- Say *please* and *thank you* when you ask for and receive something.
- Don't multitask when speaking with people, including on video calls unless otherwise agreed upon. If you must keep an eye out for something else, mention it early in the conversation, "If my phone pings, I may have to look at it as my kid's bus may be cancelled." Or, "I'm keeping an eye on email during this meeting because Ambrose should have the shipping estimate we've been waiting for, and I want to be able to share that with you."
- Take pride in your appearance. Clothes don't have to be formal or "fashionable," but they can be a clear signal that you care about yourself and support your own self-esteem. Whether you're in jeans and a hoodie or a suit and heels, make sure you feel happy and confident.
- When you are new to something, watch and listen more than you speak. It's amazing what you will learn by being an observer first.

---

38 Giving someone your sincere, open-hearted attention is one of the best gifts you can give.

- If you get nervous around people and tend to fidget or yammer, pause and breathe. Oxygen helps.
- When you have something to contribute, do. Be proud of what you know and acknowledge what you don't. It's okay if you're wrong or someone disagrees with you—that's when some of the best, most rewarding conversations start.

Understanding the expected manners within any culture is important because using them well helps mitigate surprising, unexpected situations.[39] It's up to you to notice and ask about manners. If you work in a field that requires international travel, the manners you are expected to use in one country may be very different from those in another. It's considered bad luck to stand on the threshold of a Mongolian yurt. In the United Arab Emirates, generosity is prized and guests are welcomed in a home; rejecting such hospitality is inconsiderate. *Not* slurping your soup can be considered rude in Japan. Recognizing differences in manners and customs helps us connect well with people and sets the stage for rewarding communication.

If you are reading this book, it's likely that you are not out to be a traveling oaf. It's likely you want to work well with other humans no matter the differences in cultural customs. It is the responsibility of everyone within a system to acknowledge their role in putting people at ease by recognizing and using culturally expected manners.[40] Then we can work together more effectively.

You may be thinking some norms of a culture can be odd or alienating. That may be true. Manners and mores can be and are updated all the time. It is the *spirit* of manners that matters. Manners show respect and courtesy for yourself and other humans and foster better, more adaptable interpersonal connection. They make working with humans better and less stressful.

---

39 Post Senning, Daniel., Post, Lizzie. Emily Post's Etiquette, The Centennial Edition. United States: Clarkson Potter/Ten Speed, 2022. This (very readable) book will level up your manners game for sure.

40 Some cultural expectations about "manners" are just means of control—they don't apply to the whole of a culture: one set of rules for you, another set for me. That idea of manners restricts humanity. Good manners are to be used equally by and for everyone.

Kindness is an underrated quality in workplaces in the U.S. It is often inaccurately equated with being weak or "nice." Kindness is about goodwill, benevolence, and concern for the well-being of others. Kindness gives people the benefit of the doubt. It is the attitude and action that we're all in this together and that everyone is worthy of being seen as an equal human. To behave like this requires focus and courage—it can be hard to be open-hearted with others. You can be kind and use good manners while *also* being clear and direct—this is especially important when working with humans. You can have an opinion about a project or method, state a boundary that needs to be respected, be directive about a task that must be completed, *and* say *no* to something *while* being kind. Kindness is not a one-way action that you focus only on others. You can be kind to others while also being kind to yourself. Manners and kindness are not just for the humans you work with—they are for you, too. They work together so you can communicate well. They are essential for the next Key Behavior: Be of Help.

2. Be of Help

> Think about a time you helped someone. Remember it in as much detail as you can. What was the circumstance? What time of year was it? When everything was done and your help was appreciated, how did you feel? How did the person you were helping feel? Even if the task was unpleasant or dull, you likely felt a sense of satisfaction as a result of being of help.

What comes to mind when you think of the word *help*? Help can be used in an imploring, commanding, pleading, and questioning way. Like *yes* and *no*, help is profoundly powerful as a single-word sentence: *help*. It's an extraordinary word.

At work, and in many aspects of life, help can also be a loaded word. Citizens in the United States, for example, prize rugged individualism, and there is a popular myth that people can be "self-made," which implies that needing help is a sign of laziness or ineptitude.

This can make asking a considerate question like, "Would you like some help?" tricky because part of the unspoken expectation is that the person will respond, "That's okay. I'm all set." We expect people to say *no* to our offer of help. Then we're off the hook. The perfunctory obligation of manners has been met.

But this is not what people truly hope for. It's not the true expectation. It's what we settle for.

That's why the second of the Key Behaviors—Be of Help—is so important. Being of help is an essential piece of how we make both being human and working with humans better. When you make an offer of help using your Character Compass, the Core Questions, and the Four Things to Do Forever, you offer help in a way that feels easy and confident, and sincere.

Try this: When you're in the shopping or business district in your town, look for a place with a fair number of customers and heavy or awkward doors. Make a point of opening or holding the door for others. Without being overt in your helpfulness, experiment: smile and say, "Let me get that for you" as you open or hold the door for someone.

Notice how many people acknowledge you and how many don't. Notice whether they are surprised by your helpfulness or even your manners and kindness. Sort the responses by age group. Notice if anyone returns the favor. Notice how you feel when someone says, "Thank you." Be well-mannered and kind no matter what response you receive. How does it feel to Be of Help?

An Important Point in Discussing Ways to *Be of Help*

Let's shine a bright light on a discriminatory bias associated with the concept of help: people who identify as women are often expected to help more at work. Whether it's taking the group lunch order or handling awkward conversations between colleagues, women are the default for taking on extra work and emotional labor. This is *not* the type of help we're talking about.

Sexism dictates that people, roles, and tasks labeled "female" ("women's work") are equated with a lack of power and are of minimal importance in the day-to-day operations of the business world. Tasks like helping or nurturing are marked as weak and irrelevant to the "real"— i.e., prescriptively masculine—work related to productivity and success. One of the many unfortunate aspects of this view is that it inhibits our awareness of the value of being of help at work. While this form of sexism is hurtful to women and how our contributions are perceived, it is also deeply limiting to men who risk scorn and shame if they ask for help or offer help in a way that is perceived as too nurturing or soft—i.e., prescriptively feminine.[41]

This can feel like a lot to juggle when you're trying to read this book and figure out how to deal with your colleagues more easily. If you'd like a different label for Being of Help, call it Being of Service.

Being of service can have different meanings to different people— think of being of service to your country, family, faith, school, or community. There is also an entire world known as the service industry: hoteliers, hospitality personnel, food service workers, customer service staff, and on and on. If you have one of these jobs or callings, your level of being of service to others is amplified. Being of service is another way

---

41 The term "soft skills" is inaccurate, insulting, and ineffective. Dealing with humans is hard work and the Patriarchy of Productivity doesn't want to do it. So it slaps the label "soft" onto the nuanced complexity of interpersonal skills, equates "soft" with feminine, and makes these skills less valuable in the "hard" work of Business. When was the last time you got *anything* done without other people? You're reading this book because working with humans is HARD. My recommendation: stop using the term "soft skills." Use *interpersonal, communication,* or *relational skills* instead. Better yet, just say *business skills*. It will set you free and elevate the skill of working with humans to its proper place: as the foundation of everything.

to be of help, but, at the end of the day, what we expect of each other is to show up and help get stuff done. Good communication is what helps us get stuff done with more clarity and ease.

Being of Help at Work
Helping can look like offering to carry supplies for your colleague as they hurry to give a presentation, helping someone learn how to operate a new piece of equipment, asking your desk-mate if you can get her a sandwich when you're grabbing lunch, picking up a prescription for a less-mobile colleague, etc. Being of Help is a willingness to notice the humans you work with and offer your time and effort because it's a generous thing to do. Note that it's not only about doing the things that are helpful because you have to or are ordered to, it's about doing these things because you are *willing* to.

Willingness is vital to working well with humans, even if you don't always love the idea. It's vital because it allows for connection. If you offer help willingly and don't complain about it afterward, that becomes part of your character. This doesn't mean that you must volunteer for everything or that being of service must be the thing that gets you out of bed in the morning—it's not a primary motivator for everyone. That's okay. Just notice, offer, and then help. Being helpful is another thing that, if you do it every day with sincere intention, your life and your work life will be easier. Humans like it—and you are human.

You may be thinking, "If I help all the time I'm never going to get ahead because people will expect that I'm always the person who's going to do everything." Or, "If I help them, this team is never going to figure out how to do things on their own." That's not necessarily the case. While it's true that if you are a doormat and are not clear about the difference between being taken advantage of and being helpful, you will likely miss opportunities for development. Doing your team's work for them is ineffective, but showing them where to find the information to gain new skills can be a more helpful path. Despite what many elite business schools will tell you, succeeding at work is not a zero-sum game. If you are of help and deliver that help in ways that build sincere relationships with your colleagues, you become known as someone who is interested in everyone's success—including your own.

That's why Being of Help is a Key Behavior in working with humans. But sometimes you may not know what to do or how to assist. This can be especially true if the person or situation you'd like to help with is dealing with a crisis. The easiest thing to do when you don't know how to help is to make use of the other tools in your toolkit. Helping, especially when you're uncertain about what to do, is a perfect time to connect to your Character Compass. As you notice what help may be needed, if you're connected to your character, your curiosity and choices for action will likely be more grounded and confident.

How to Help:
1. **Notice**. What's happening around you? Who or what needs help? You don't have to wait for a crisis; pitch in, it's friendlier.
2. **Ask**. Is help needed or wanted? You can ask while starting to help: helping someone carry something heavy or offering assistance when they have forgotten someone's name in the middle of an introduction. But check yourself: are you helping or are you critiquing and taking over? Keep in mind that you are a *partner* in helping.
3. **Offer**. Saying, "Here is what I can do to help," or, "I will give it my best," tells the person whom you are offering to help what you are able to do. Ensure clarity.
4. **Complete**. *Do* what you said you would do. Follow through. Don't forget or neglect your commitment.
5. **Close**. Follow up and close the loop. "Hey, I just finished putting those boxes together for shipment. They are ready to get picked up by FedEx." This builds confidence all around and promotes trust. Look for other helpers and be a helper for others (thank you, Mr. Rogers.[42])

When *you* need help—you're moving to a new place, you're cooking dinner for a big party, you need to have your car worked on but don't

---

[42] Head, Barry., Rogers, Fred. Mister Rogers Talks with Parents. United States: Berkley Books, 1983.

have a mechanic—where do you go for assistance? Do you ask people who won't be timely or useful, or do you ask reliable people who are interested in helping you in an effective way? Unless you like to be frustrated, you choose the helpful, reliable people.

Your coworkers have the same attitude: they are looking for reliable assistance. That's true whether they need information or effort. When you are a person who can be helpful and resourceful in a way that supports your colleagues and upholds your values, you increase your reputation and character. Do that while communicating well and being kind, and you add humanity into your workplace. Be a person who is willing to do a job, be responsible for it, and do it in a respectful way. Many people think that this combination of traits is like finding a unicorn in a haystack. But there are any number of you unicorns hanging out in haystacks everywhere. This work will help you get to know each other and create something magical.

By actively putting yourself in the position to be helpful in the best way you can, you display your willingness to be of service to others. That's what employers and colleagues want and often don't ask for—not only that you are able, but also that you show up and willingly use your abilities. The bonus is that when you are helpful, you feel good about yourself as well.

This brings us to the next thing on the list of Key Behaviors: Have Pride in Your Work.

3. Have Pride in Your Work

You have good manners and you are willing to be of help. Now we need to tackle the third thing: Have Pride in Your Work. This is HUGE. It is also the biggest source of strife and confusion among different generations at work. It's the source of the battle between the attitudes of "the problem with you kids today …" and "okay, Boomer…" Differing age-based perceptions of how younger people and older people approach life and work are not new.

> **The trouble with youths today ...**
> "Our youths love luxury. They have bad manners, contempt for authority—they show disrespect for their elders and love to chatter in place of exercise. Children are now tyrants, not the servants of their households. They no longer rise when their elders enter the room. They contradict their parents, chatter before company, gobble up food, and tyrannize teachers."   —*attributed to (but likely not) Socrates, 469-399 B.C.E.*[43]

What we have here is a classic (if not ancient Greek) version of, "Hey, you kids! Get off my lawn!" Essentially, the complaint about Boomers being hoodlums, Gen-Xers being slackers, and Millennials being entitled brats has been around for centuries.

---

43 This oft-cited quote was probably written in the nineteen hundreds, but the essence of its complaint is clear: *Change is scary and youths can be irritating.* Fair enough. Also consider that a) change is central to life, b) irritations often have elements of miscommunication and unclear expectations at their core, c) you were once a youth, and d) lawns are fun to play on. If you'd like a Greek philosopher's actual thoughts on the temperament of youth, see Aristotle's *Art of Rhetoric*, Book II, Chapter 12 (4th century B.C.E). The chapter is not really a complaint, but an examination of the fact that younger people generally haven't experienced as many hardships as older people due to less time being alive.

Every generation has a form of recalcitrant, lazy, and irreverent behavior. But it's not *all* they do—easy labels and stereotypes are never the whole story. What this quote gets at is that younger people often fail to meet expectations. You may be trying to do something similar when you complain about your coworkers. ***The question you must always ask is: Do my colleagues know what my expectations are, and can I explain and discuss them clearly?*** If the other humans don't know your expectations, you likely didn't take the time to understand them yourself, tell others what they are, and have a conversation about why your expectations are important to the project at hand.

Doing things well and becoming proud of the quality of your work feels good. The trouble with old people today (by "old" I mean anyone over 45) is that we're horrible at talking about how to do work in a way that demonstrates pride. Sometimes we discuss it in terms of consistency and brand, "Is this on-brand?" Having pride in your work *does* build your brand, if we think in marketing terms. But when we look beyond the promotional aspect of work and include our values, we build reputation and character. Where to begin? With context and conversation, of course.

Imagine that everything that you do at work—every email, text message, phone call, meeting—is something that you must physically create and hold to use. Each item's quality reflects your skill, your talent, your craft, and your name. Let's also imagine that none of those things must be complicated or etched with gold, they simply must work well and not fall to pieces if you set one on a coffee table.

If all those things were physical objects, aside from being aware of your need for a much bigger desk, how would you feel about the quality of what you produce every day? If everything you said and did was easily identified as something that you physically made and was measured by its quality, would you feel proud of your work?

When people make physical things like cars, clothing, toilet paper, microchips, furniture, candles, food, tractors, etc., there is a physical interaction between the person doing the work and the products they create. The pride with which they create objects can be *felt* and physically observed. The quality of whatever work you do—the way you communicate, show up on time, proof your emails, complete your tasks—shows that you have pride in your work in the same way as someone who builds a physical product.

The details matter. They show you are paying attention to your projects and to the people you work with and for. Attending to details shows that you can meet the basic expectations of your work and that you can do your job well.

The Age We Live In—A Substantial and Important Tangent
The foundations of workplace expectations were grown in the Industrial Age and are deeply tied to U.S. national history.[44] These expectations are such an integrated part of what we do that we, for better and for worse, don't even know they are there. They're like the air we breathe.

Complaints about intergenerational communication are a core example of workplace expectations that have blended into the background of our day-to-day so much that we don't know how to discuss them. Every day, someone publishes another article about how Boomer bosses are frustrated by Millennial or Gen Z employees because they have to tell them about things like how to behave in business meetings. If people are brand-new to being employed, why would they know how a boss wants them to behave? Conversely, why do younger employees become dismissive if Boomers don't know about the most recent tech tools? Cloud storage and server integration are not always topics of conversation. **The experiences we're individually comfortable with are the things we assume everyone else knows.**

One of the most frequent complaints I hear is about whether someone is "working hard." How do we define "hard work" when so much variability in generational experience is in play? These terms are different for different people in different jobs, as they should be. The hard work required to build a house is distinctive from that required to write a screenplay. The hard work needed to create a website is different from the hard work needed to manage a city-wide food pantry.

---

44 Expectations of the Industrial Age also apply to North America and the Westernized world at large.

So why is some hard work valued more than other types? That is a huge question with many important answers that are deeply connected, but its root is tied to how we privilege the perception of work that can be seen as "productive" in the Industrial sense. Our assumptions about how people are supposed to work hard were established with a pre-Information Age mindset: the value of what you can produce, consistently, without error or delay equates to your value as a worker. That's true, but it's not the whole story. The whole story includes the human being who is doing the work—and that is a whole lot less predictable.

Examine just a few of the variables in the generations below:

Generation	Workplace Background	Notable Humans
The Greatest Generation/GI Generation b. 1901–1924	The Greatest Generation is revered for their resilience, physical labor in service to country, and self-sacrifice during WWII. Their shared work ethic, post-war victory mindset, and dedication to productivity are the foundations for how United States companies operate.	Rosa Parks, Louis Armstrong, Jimmy Stewart, Frida Kahlo, James Baldwin, Jack LaLanne, Betty White, Rosie the Riveter
The Silent Generation b. 1925–1945	Silent Generation and Baby Boomers also associate physical productivity and labor as beneficial; the victory over fascism in WWII reinforced that productivity is a noble means to success.	Gloria Steinem, Mick Jagger, Mel Brooks, Bob Dylan, Neil Armstrong, Justice Sandra Day O'Connor, Dr. Martin Luther King, Jr.
Baby Boomers b. 1946–1963		Oprah Winfrey, Cornel West, Sec. Hillary Rodham Clinton, Steve Jobs, President Barack Obama, Yo-Yo Ma, Prince ⚥

Gen-X b. 1964-ish– 1980-ish	Gen-X is a bridge between the Industrial and Information Ages. Their first jobs were generally mechanical or service-based: waiting tables, working an assembly line, mowing lawns, housekeeping in a hotel, etc. Digital information technology became more of an influence and was more mainstream by their second or third jobs with the internet and email becoming commonplace in the 1990s.	Dave Grohl, Tina Fey, Chris Rock, Jack Dorsey, Julian and Joaquin Castro, Sara Blakely, Snoop Dogg, Salma Hayek, Ethan Hawke
Millennials/Gen Y b. 1980-ish– 2000-ish	Millennials' work is more likely to be technology- or information-oriented from the start of their employment history. Gen-Z has been born digital and their work can be completely oriented to digital and virtual space.	Emma Stone, Rafael Nadal, Malala Yousafzai, Rihanna, Elliot Page, Alexandria Ocasio-Cortez, Kizzmekia Corbett, PhD
Gen Z/ Gen Alpha b. 2000ish– present		Greta Thunberg, Billie Eilish, Gavin Grimm, Olivia Rodrigo, David Hogg, Lil Naz X, Zendaya

Each generation has a different experience of what hard work means, but none of us are very good at defining those experiences and their associated expectations for other humans. Multiple generations working together is common and great, but since we don't discuss our different frames of reference, it's no wonder we're flummoxed by what we expect of each other at work.

∞

Discussions about having pride in your work can feel antiquated, like a relic from the Industrial Age, unhelpfully tied to fixation on productivity. In our Information Age, the volume and complexity of what we create are vastly different than when we made mostly physical objects, but the expectation of quality still matters. This requires you to pay attention to every one of your actions. That can seem like a lot. Guess what? It is.

When our jobs are comprised of meetings, sending endless strings of emails, posting on social media, writing proposals, managing spreadsheets, creating "content," and trying to do all of these things at lightning speed, it's hard to know if you are creating a quality product. It's hard to know if your proposal has an impact, let alone whether what you post on social media does. With so much information to take in and produce, it's difficult to monitor the quality of each individual message. It's easy to think that the specific quality of what you said, posted, or added up doesn't matter. It's easy to think that punctuation doesn't matter or that you don't have to pay attention when there's so much going on all the time.

It's easy to think that, but it creates problems for your pride.

Does it take time to pay attention to the quality of emails that you send? Yes. Does it take time to consider, when you write a post on a social media platform, what impact your words may have on another person? Yes. Does it take time to pause and remember that attuning to your character and communication is a way you can show pride in your work and in yourself? Yes, it does. And it's worth it because it helps you to share your awareness of the humanity within yourself and others. It adds a glow of pride to all of your communication.

4. Don't Be a Jackass[45]

> "Be the change you want to see in the world."
> —*not* Mahatma Gandhi[46]

Jackass *(noun):* a person who chooses to engage in any manner of behaviors that are rude, obtuse, harmful, corrupt, or obnoxious.

> BIG IMPORTANT NOTE: *This last Key Behavior is the most important.* It's the one that I mentioned at the start as the behavior we need **not** to do. It's meant to be a helpful hint, not a punitive scold. "Don't be a jackass" is usually uttered with a fair amount of force and venom. That's *not* the tone here. Imagine it as part of the reminders you may hear or say when leaving the house: *remember your wallet ...have a nice day ...don't be a jackass* ...The stuff that helps us get through the day. Please remember that a joyful, open-hearted laugh is the shortest distance between people.

The statement "Don't Be a Jackass" is meant as a reality check. *Jackassedness is a type of behavior—the combined manifestation of an absence of curiosity, a shortage of empathy, and a profound disinterest in anything*

---

[45] On the choice of the term *Jackass*: Technically, a jackass is a male donkey; a jenny, or jennet, is a female donkey. But in our culture, the term *jackass* itself is not as gender-biased as other terms, i.e., someone being a *dick* or a *bitch*. Whatever our gender, all humans are equal in our ability to display jackassed behavior.

[46] Gandhi said many things that are similar to this statement, but not *exactly* this. This quote has been attributed to many people through the years, hence, "*not* Mahatma Gandhi."

other than one's own immediate experience. Reminding yourself not to be a jackass helps you evaluate your actions when you feel the pull toward the grim combination of behaviors (interrupting people when they speak, using positional power as an excuse for condescension, ignoring the people who helped you along your path once they are no longer of use) that perpetuate the all-too-common workplace routines of self-absorption and neglect of the greater good.

Why, then, is the fourth thing "Don't *Be* a Jackass" rather than "Don't *Behave* Like a Jackass"? Two reasons: 1) "Don't Be a Jackass" has a better ring to it, and 2) because it's a quick check on your own emotional disposition and thought processes. If you behave like a jackass, you are probably thinking like one—you are viewing the world through a jackassed lens. The neuroscientific basis of habit formation tells us that if you think a certain way long enough, thoughts tend to become part of your reality.[47] Essentially, if you behave and think like a jackass, a jackass you shall become. Think of "Don't Be a Jackass" as a prayer, talisman, or mantra of sorts for what you hope *not* to be.

Jackassedness—the über-view

A grave misconception in much of current business culture is that if you are not being aggressive, tough, or on-guard, people will take advantage of you. You must *watch your back*, *cover your ass*, and *protect what's yours*. It is a zero-sum, fearful, and harmfully competitive approach to the world. Work cultures tend to promote the idea that if you give a person an inch, they'll take a mile. It's a paranoid and very exhausting *they-are-out-to-get-me* mentality. If you treat people like you expect them to manipulate you or take advantage of you, at some point they probably will. This is because you may be inspiring jackassedness in others.

If, however, you are direct, kind, and forthright with people—which does not mean you are a nearsighted idealist—they will more likely treat you in a similar way because you have used good manners, been helpful, had pride in the quality of your actions, and thus have not been a jackass.

---

[47] Damasio, Antonio. Descartes' Error: Emotion, Reason, and the Human Brain. United Kingdom: Penguin Publishing Group, 2005, 162.

Example: The Spinach Test

Sometimes the kindest thing you can do for someone is tell them there is a problem. You can always find a way to do so with respect for the person's humanity. For example: you could tell a friend that he has spinach stuck in his teeth in a way that makes you a total jackass: point and laugh, insult his hygiene, and watch his embarrassment grow and his trust in you evaporate. Or you could help the guy out by kindly telling him about the spinach, decreasing his embarrassment, and increasing his trust in you. You also won't have to walk around with your friend and hope he doesn't smile.

Not being a jackass does not mean that you are a sap, indecisive, gullible, or that you avoid challenging interactions with other humans. It means that you can be confident, authoritative, and powerful *while* being courteous, helpful, and confidence-inspiring. It's not an either/or choice.

Calmness and curiosity are the natural foes of jackass behavior.
While Don't Be a Jackass is the last of the four Key Behaviors, if you think you can skip it, it's likely that you aren't doing the first three very well. Each of these ideas supports each other, just as each of the Essential Tools intertwine. Sometimes, if you're cranky or mad or hurt by a person or situation, it's hard to have good manners or be helpful or behave in a way that will support your character. That's when you can invoke the mantra *"Don't Be a Jackass"* and let it repeat on a quiet, persistent loop in your head while breathing deeply and fortifying yourself against the jackassed urge to spit tacks.

Sometimes, if situations are unpleasant enough—especially with coworkers or bosses who have not yet had the good fortune of learning about the Key Behaviors—it can take all your energy not to do something equally unpleasant in response. That struggle is fine. The moment of frustration or furiousness will pass and you can draw on manners and pride and helpfulness to move forward and respect your own boundaries (as in, "I hear what you're saying; I'm going to go elsewhere and think before I respond"). Every day, we have to deal with events and humans that will make us feel vexed. How we choose to perceive and respond to those situations is entirely up to us. We can react with defensive or hostile, jackassed behavior ("Well, nobody told *me* the deadline changed," or "Screw you! I was protecting the goals of the company!"), or we can use the Key Behaviors and have a better time ensuring that the goals of the work and our own integrity are maintained. They combine with all the other tools to support both the way you work with humans and the success we can all have in creating better workplace experiences.

The Limbo vs. Pole Vaulting

As you look back at the Key Behaviors, you may think, "Sharing manners and kindness, being of help, having pride in one's work, not being a jackass—these things are so basic. Is the bar really set *that low* in the workplace?" Yes, it is. What matters here is not the height of the bar, but your approach to it. It's the difference between doing the Limbo and pole vaulting. Both have bars that need to be cleared, but if you apply the Limbo skillset to pole vaulting or vice versa, you miss the point of the activity. It's easy to do the Limbo under a pole vaulting bar.

That's how many people think about manners, being of help, and their own reputation. They don't notice their circumstances and think they don't have to. They use manners in the situational equivalent of walking under a pole-vaulting bar, and think they have been successful. What they've been is a jackass.

The most basic example is the shopping cart test: when you use a shopping cart to carry your items to the car, do you return the cart to a central location like the front of the store or the cart stall in the parking lot? It's an easy, kind thing to do, so why is it so tempting to leave it for someone else to manage? Jackassery is tempting. You must try not to succumb! Take back your cart and do the world a solid.

Rude, obtuse, harmful, corrupt, or obnoxious behavior is often abundant at work. People steal each other's ideas, interrupt each other in meetings, lie about the status of projects, build things that have known detrimental impact, deliberately sidestep the law, undermine others' successes, and microwave fish in the office kitchen.

Why don't we talk about what *not* to do? Why do we avoid conversations that we think should be obvious? We assume that people will know. That approach is not working very well, and it's doing all of us a disservice.

My Epiphany About Not Being a Jackass
The inconvenient thing about the Key Behavior of Don't Be a Jackass is how deceptively simple it is. It came to me early in my management career, while working at a four-star resort in Vermont: Topnotch at Stowe. In the early 1990s, massage therapy was moving into the mainstream, but most of the U.S. was relatively new to the concept of massage therapy. The thought of being touched in a therapeutic, non-sexual way was still a weird idea for many people, so most spas had "How to Spa" brochures—elaborate, expensively printed pamphlets that would describe every aspect of what guests were supposed to do to enjoy their time at the spa. Now you'd just look at the FAQ section of a resort's webpage.

But what our stressed-out, often demanding guests needed most was the one thing that the lengthy brochure neglected to state: what NOT to do. We didn't tell them because we assumed that they would *know* what not to do. That was a mistake. The stereotypes of disrespectful behavior of the affluent toward the "help" were occasionally true, and being specific about what was not acceptable behavior could have been as useful as instructions for how to stay hydrated in the sauna.

The same could be said for the employee training manual about guest service. It gave lengthy descriptions of how to comport oneself and provide seamless hospitality experiences, but it also made assumptions about the behaviors employees should just *know* to avoid. Employees had a benefit that guests did not: we had time to practice how to do things well and course-correct if we were about to make a mistake or create a problem for each other or our guests.

The huge moment of clarity came one day when I was having to deal with both an obnoxious guest and an irritating employee. The guest was behaving rudely to a massage therapist, and the employee was behaving badly to a coworker. I was attempting to refer them to their appropriate document, spa brochure or training manual, and to fix both situations with as little drama as possible. Bad behavior was the root of both problems. After spending way too much energy having to address these incidents, I returned to the spa office and collapsed in my desk chair.

The manager I trusted most, Danny, was working on the staff schedule.[48] He looked at me and recognized the sense of futility that comes from having to talk about behaviors that you know people should not be doing.

I pointed to the long-winded brochure and elaborate manual and sighed, "All these steps could be boiled down to the things people *shouldn't* do in a spa."

Danny gave a wry smile and said, "Step One: Don't Be a Jackass."

I laughed and added, "Step Two: Commit to Step One."

In that moment, my career of working to improve workplaces through better communication was born. While it's pithy and true that those two steps will get you a long way toward working well with other humans, the past three decades have taught me that there is an additional

---

48 This is his real name!

step needed to make the first two stick. It requires both humanity and compassion. I have, quite originally, labeled it Step Three:

Remember That Not Being a Jackass Is More Difficult Than It Seems

That's the truth that dwells under the deceptive simplicity of Don't Be a Jackass: it's difficult. The difficulty lies in the behavioral assumptions and the inherent structural flaws in how our organizations are designed—in their deliberate inhumanity. When we must produce to prove our worth, when we operate in a system that looks at moment-to-moment fluctuations in data from sources that vary from the S&P 500 to celebrity social media feeds without thinking of including long-term impact or meaning, it's challenging to remember that our behavior affects the humans around us. We know we should think beyond our noses, beyond parking-lot cart corrals and microwaved lunches, but the rewards for doing what we want right now are immediate. The rewards for consideration, communication, and choosing to engage one's character take longer to see, but the effort is worth it. It requires emotional presence and curiosity, vulnerability, and clumsiness—and it requires that you care. Most of all, it requires your humanity.

Authenticity and Being Yourself at Work

Authenticity has become a popular word. But when everything you can purchase or say or do is labeled as *authentic, true,* or *real,* the concept of authenticity can sound like bullshit. When it comes to your behavior when working with humans, it's important that you look beyond buzzwords and align yourself with your character. (Which is easier to do when you use your Character Compass.)

Part of the power of the Key Behaviors rests in their sincerity. Without sincerity, your behavior becomes fluff and can drift toward jackassery. That said, there are times when you may feel you have to fake the Key Behaviors to get yourself through a boring meeting or an awkward conversation. That's fine. If you are feeling like it's a stretch to be of help, kind manners may be an easier option. If you are feeling like the momentum of a project is dragging to a standstill, you can move things along by offering help in a sincere way that doesn't take over or bulldoze the process.

Emotional awareness, regulation, and dexterity are huge assets when working with humans. Your awareness of and respect for your own humanity is essential for your ability to acknowledge and respect it in others.

In workplaces where humanity is not respected, there can be a yearning to "speak your truth" or be a "truth-teller" or some similar label that means you are fed-up with being treated in a way that feels bad. When this desire to have your humanity and personal experience acknowledged breaks free, there can be a lot of energy behind it—and this can create an unexpected conversation. The unfortunate result in many such workplaces is that your good observations about things that are wrong, problematic, or inefficient get lost in the translation between a valid point and an emotional reaction. In these situations, your Character Compass is indispensable because it can help you perceive your emotions and communicate them in a way that is aligned with your character, is truthful, *and* can be heard by others. It will help you to cultivate emotional responsibility and regulation in order to have constructive communication at work. That's important because when you are working with others it is vital to remember: they are there *with* you, not *for* you. We're all in this together.

That's why knowing how to connect to your Character Compass, use the Communication Must-Haves, and practice the Key Behaviors is so useful: each tool helps you to perceive and use your emotions to inform your actions and feel like yourself while working with others. All the tools in this book help you speak and act *for* your emotions rather than *from* them.[49]

When you connect to your character and make choices based on your values, emotional presence—your ability to notice and be informed by your emotions without feeling overwhelmed by them—becomes easier. That's also why it's important to reconnect to the First Assignment at the beginning of this book. How do you want to feel at work? Ask yourself and use all the other tools to help you do so authentically, even when it seems like a lot of effort. When you're doing all these things, you are being yourself at work. *That's* authenticity.

---

49 The distinction between speaking *for* instead of *from* emotions is priceless. Speaking *for* emotions can sound like, "Part of me feels angry about the way this team is interacting and avoiding the topic of responsibility; let's discuss your next steps now." Speaking *from* emotions can sound like, "You are all making me so angry and are acting like children! I can't stand how you're not just getting this done!" For more information on speaking for emotions rather than from them, see Schwartz, Richard C., Internal Family Systems Therapy. United States: Guilford Publications, 2013.

Unexpected Conversations:
The Key Behaviors

A vast majority of the unexpected conversations you have at work relate to the Key Behaviors: someone didn't do the thing you expected them to, and now you must talk to them about it and figure out what to do next.

Maybe your colleague's manners are rusty, maybe they didn't proofread an email, maybe they don't follow through with the help they offer, or maybe they have been a jackass. These are the conversations where you must be very aware and deliberate and use the tools in this book. It's very tempting to meet jackassery with jackassery. Don't do it.[50] If you are feeling frustrated or reactive:

- Go slowly and make sure you can breathe. *Inhale, exhale, repeat* ...
- Connect to your Character Compass as you breathe and ask:
  - Which value is closest at hand? Start with the one that helps you feel at ease most readily.
  - When you breathe, think, and feel simultaneously and on purpose, you have access to your humanity—and it's easier to see it in others, even when they are annoying.
- Consider the Four Things to Do Forever
  - Those four steps help you decrease the reactivity in the situation by intentionally adding curiosity to the mix.

The unexpected conversations that you must have about not being a jackass are difficult because you hope you'll never have to have them. You cross your fingers and pray your colleagues will be generous, emotionally well-regulated humans. That's a nice thing to hope for and, as I've mentioned, hope is a form of planning—but it's only the beginning. Hope and then build the scaffolding to make your hope come to life.

---

50 There were a few times in my management career where I probably should have fired myself for being too quick with a snarky response toward an infuriating colleague—I still regret each one. But I didn't have this book and wasn't as grounded in my character as I am today. You are already far more prepared than most.

To be successful when talking about unexpected jackassery, talk about it *a lot* BEFORE it happens. Have conversations about how *not* to be a jackass when it's easy and everyone is lovely, i.e., not being a jackass. Don't put yourself in the position of having to deal with it on the fly without any practice.

Talk about jackassery when you're onboarding a new employee. "At Acme Corporation, we openly discuss expectations and behaviors. Here's what we want of each other, and here's what we don't." Have conversations about character at team get-togethers. Share your favorite tool from this book over tea or a beer. Be a standard for infusing humanity into your work, and you'll head off some jackassery before it happens. And you know what I'm about to say: all this does require you to practice.

Practice With a Pal:
The Key Behaviors

When you start a new project or work with a new team, talk about the Key Behaviors with everyone. Look back to your First Assignment and to your Expectations Inventory. You can use that structure to frame the conversation and set expectations about shared behaviors. If you create and discuss expectations at the beginning of a project, you create a point of reference that you can refer to if jackassery shows up.

> **Talking about behaviors before they become annoying or problematic is its own diabolically unexpected and fabulous way to bring humanity into working with humans.**

You can practice with a pal, or, if you're feeling like you want to jump in and go for it, practice in a kick-off meeting, a weekly meeting, or even on a Monday-morning huddle. Start by asking any of the following questions—or add your own!

- "As we work on this project, in what ways can we offer help to each other?"
    - How do we want to acknowledge helpfulness when it happens?
        - *"I noticed that Andrea stepped in and helped to make sure the new addendum was added to the quarterly report in time to send it to the review board. Your work reduced everyone's stress load. Thank you, Andrea."*
- "What does doing a good job on this project look like?"
    - What will you be most proud of when this project is done?
        - *"The project has been going on for what feels like eons and compromising quality would have been easy. The fact that everyone has shown pride in the quality of our work at every step means everything to the integrity of our brand."*

- Are there temptations to cut corners? What corners specifically?
  - *"We could have shipped all those samples... the color was so close to being right. I'm glad we redid them–the client was amazed with how they looked!"*
- **"What's the kindest thing that you've noticed people doing for each other lately?"**[51]
  - What are the little things that we do for each other that you really appreciate?
    - *"Julie, you know I get overwhelmed at the start of new projects and you always send a text to say you believe in me. Your encouragement gets me through my initial jitters. Thank you!"*
    - *"Thanks for holding the door. It means a lot."*
- **"How would you like to feel about how we interact?"**
  - Remember a time when a project or meeting went _well_? Describe what was happening.
  - Describe it and capture the big ideas of what felt good about it.
    - *"The whole team was excited, even though some of us were nervous, too. We had a clear plan and were really interested in starting something new."*
  - Remember a time when a project or a meeting went _poorly_? Describe what was happening.
  - Describe it and capture the big themes of what didn't work.
    - *"It felt like we were being put on the spot for losing a contract we had no control over. Nothing was resolved and we just couldn't find a way to make it work. The apathy was exhausting."*
  - As we work together, let's strive for more of what went well and feels good (often the three Key Behaviors), and let's stop and

---

51 Cynicism check: If you find yourself thinking something like, "The kindest thing I've noticed is that they do their jobs and leave me alone," stop for a second. As you may have guessed, I'm generally in favor of a witty retort, but notice if your first thought *feels* spiteful or too sharp—it may be a sign of cynicism's alluring pull. Resist! It's okay to notice and offer yourself kindness. And it's a delightfully human thing to do.

correct our actions as we're re-creating what went poorly (often jackass behavior).

- When things are going well or going poorly, what's the kindest, clearest way to notice it?
  - *"Hey this meeting went really well. Thanks for being willing to share your thoughts constructively."*
- What will we do to acknowledge the good and the bad and make changes as needed?
  - *"Okay, well, that experiment taught us that we <u>never</u> want to do anything like it again. Let's do an after-action review and see what we did well and what we need to watch for in the future. Let's learn from this and carry on."*

Can you imagine if the people you worked with could ask, answer, and then follow through on these questions? It's pretty amazing when it happens. You just have to start—and then …practice.

What's in It for YOU
and how do you know if it's working?

Using the Key Behaviors and Adjusting as Needed

Here is a quick way of knowing whether the Key Behaviors are absent: everyone is complaining about everything and everyone. Cynicism is high and your team's humanity is hiding in the corner, hoping for the day when the oppressive weight of disappointment and alienation will end. Perky, huh?

When the Key Behaviors are present, people communicate clearly, are hopeful and generous, and mostly enjoy themselves—even if the work is difficult.

When you look at your organization, your team, or even the conversations you practice with a pal, try your best to see both the behaviors that are problems and those that are assets. Those that are assets can be developed and infused with humanity as you work with other humans.

Look at each list in the table below and add your own examples, detailing what you notice as present or absent with each Key Behavior. There are myriad ways these behaviors manifest every day. The important part is that you *notice* the Key Behaviors in action. This will encourage you to practice more!

Manners and Kindness Are Present:	Manners and Kindness Are Absent:
Conversations are cooperative. *Differing perspectives are asked for and appreciated.*	Conversations are combative and defensive. *Being "right" is a coveted position and someone is always a "winner."*
Colleagues are respectful with their words and actions. *Even when energy is high and ideas are flying around, people don't talk over each other, and everyone feels heard.*	Interruption and dismissiveness is the norm. *Any idea that disrupts established rules is degraded or ignored.*
There is a sense of trust and psychological safety among colleagues. *It's okay to take risks and participate.* *Effort is respected and growth is encouraged.*	Microaggressions and disrespect abound. *No acknowledgment of or space for different human experiences.*
Listening precedes talking and people are open to information other than what they already have. *People know they can always learn something from each other.*	Disinterest in learning about others; curiosity is absent. Low situational awareness. *People are tuned-out to the needs and experiences of others.*
Even if relationships are not interpersonally close, they are sincere and courteous. *A general feeling of being welcome and included is the norm.*	Manners are perfunctory and performative: "politeness" is a checkbox, not a reality. *Insincerity abounds.*

Being Helpful Is Present:	Being Helpful Is Absent:
Active learning is supported and shame-free. *You know someone will share knowledge without judgment. You are not expected to know everything already; you are encouraged to learn more than you already know.*	"Wow …how can you not know that?" is the general, derogatory attitude toward others. *There is no room for learning, and growth is frowned upon. Curiosity is a weakness. Being a know-it-all is rewarded.*
There is a sense of shared responsibility in how work gets done. *Teamwork really does make the dream work.*	"That's not in my job description" is a default setting. *Passing the buck is commonplace. Personal responsibility is avoided at every opportunity.*
Cooperative and strategic thinking infuse conversations. *Listening and curiosity are valued because they allow people to build off shared ideas. Credit is given openly.*	Following top-down orders is the only "right" way to do something. *The leader is the only person who has the ideas. Anyone else is an idiot.*
Help is offered; help is asked for. *"We're all in this together." Being of help is seen as a remedy for feelings of fear and perfectionism.*	Help is withheld; people try to handle everything on their own. *Sink or swim and "this is what separates the men from the boys" are common attitudes.*
Curiosity leads all conversations—no one assumes they know the only way to do something. *People are open to differences in perspective and experience and how they serve common goals.*	Steamrolling or taking over is common and is often misconstrued as being helpful. *Superhero complex often combines with needing to be the smartest person in the room and thinking there is only one right way to fix a problem.*

Pride in Your Work Is Present:	Pride in Your Work Is Absent:
Thoughtful attention to detail.* *People notice the value of quality without hyper-fixating on perfection.*	Disregard for detail and nuance; no discernment of when these are needed. *"Don't worry, no one will care"—the emphasis is on what you can get away with, not on pride in what you can do well.*
Awareness of both one's own reputation and of the group's reputation as a whole. *Pride in associating with people who share a commitment to skill and quality.*	Action without consideration of impact. *Turn the crank and check the box. Routines become ruts and apathy abounds.*
Ability to notice good work in others and be a champion of their success. *Admiration of and appreciation for skill and commitment is shared openly.*	Scorn and dismissiveness of others' success. *Jealousy and superiority dominate conversations in the guise that others are inferior in their work or expression.*
Wanting to learn about your field and expand your awareness. *Experts know they can always learn something new—even from beginners.*	Hoarding knowledge and status; being anchored to a specific point in time: "Well, in my day ..." *Refusal to acknowledge that fields change and knowledge expands and deepens. Unwillingness to share expertise.*
Frank knowledge of strengths and weaknesses—knowledge of both is an asset. *Experts willingly seek the skill of others who complement their knowledge—it makes outcomes much stronger.*	Inability to accept critique or suggestion, no room for improvement. *"I have spoken. I'm the expert. You're wrong and what you're trying to do won't work."*

*You can be detailed without being perfectionistic. Perfectionism is often remedied when people know that they can help and be helped without judgment. That combination creates really good work.

People ARE NOT Being Jackasses:	People ARE Being Jackasses:
People care about and encourage shared success. A rising tide lifts all boats. *Focus on equity. People champion each other's shared and individual goals.*	Everything is zero-sum: there must always be a loser and there can only be one winner. *Everything is a competition. Status and ranking are unyielding and pervasive.*
People are valued for who they are, the skills they bring, and their interest in contributing to the whole. *Potential is recognized and supported.*	Defensive routines are attached to hurtful cultural norms: sexism, racism, ageism, ableism, etc. Systems of privilege drive decisions without acknowledgment of their own existence. *Please, fight this paradigm—it's bad for everyone! Resistance is NOT futile!*
Conflicting opinions are welcome and discussed with open attitudes. *Emotional awareness helps these conversations go well.*	Hurtful and rude attitudes are normalized. *Belligerence is a commonplace tool for avoiding disagreements.*
Focused communication and trust create highly functional and generative teams. *And that just makes work more satisfying—yay!*	Bullying and fear are common tools of "motivation." *Workplace harassment is normalized and everyone is litigious.*
Responsibility and acceptance thrive. *Generosity of spirit is the norm. Humanity is welcome and celebrated.*	Blame and shame are everywhere. *Your spirit sinks a little every day and cynicism takes root in your heart.*

THE KEY BEHAVIORS 139

The Point

What's in it for you if you get good at the Key Behaviors? Aside from the inestimable joy and delight you will feel by being a good communicator and colleague who infuses care and humanity into any work environment you enter from now until the end of time? Other than your spirit being uplifted, your interest in work rekindled, your confidence in your ability to handle all sorts of unexpected conversations, and your sense of potential for what humans can do when we pay attention and deliberately get better at working with other humans? Beyond that, not much.

Conclusion

The problems within the paradigm of productivity and their cost to our humanity can feel too big to consider as a whole. But you don't have to think about it all at once. You can be part of the solution to that bigger problem every day by using these essential tools. When you know how to work with humans, using these foundational, practical tools every day, you'll see the real difference you make in the quality of your professional relationships and interactions. You'll see how the existing production-fixated paradigm can be transformed to include our humanity. And unexpected conversations can become a valuable, manageable, and even a fairly delightful part of working with humans.

Your New Tools:

1. **Your Character Compass**
2. **The Communication Must-Haves**
   - Core Questions
   - Four Things to Do Forever
3. **The Key Behaviors**
   - Share Manners and Kindness
   - Be of Help
   - Have Pride in Your Work
   - Don't Be a Jackass

It's a simple list. It's POWERFUL and it requires thought and practice to use well. It requires that you understand your feelings and your thoughts, that you understand and share your expectations, and that you are willing to challenge those expectations. It requires compassion for yourself and other humans. It requires that you're willing to learn and reflect every day, amid project deadlines, endless busy-ness, and general jackassery. It requires you to dive in and try, no matter how clumsy you feel, and pitch in to make things better. If you can have some fun in the process, all the better.

When you're stuck or need help figuring out where to start, look at the map in this book. Find yourself on it and navigate from there. When in doubt, breathe and connect to your character. Action is easier when you know who you are and how you want to be.

Practice. Keep going. I believe in you. We can all get better at working with humans.

∞

Next Steps

What You Can Do Next:

- Review and revisit the exercises. Finish them if you skipped a few while reading.
- Do the Practice with a Pal exercises with many pals.
- Share this book with your team. (It makes a great gift.)
- Talk about it with your friends.
- And practice, practice, practice!

Go to *workingwithhumans.com* for downloads of the exercises and for more information on how you can keep building all the skills you've been exploring in this book.

Here's to you, your humanity, and the great art of Working With Humans.

A million thanks,
Laura

Navigating Your Way

The landscape of Working With Humans is varied and rich. There are beautiful opportunities and splendid vistas as well as tricky situations and spots to avoid. When you set out to build your skills and knowledge and then share your experiences with others, it makes for a wonderful adventure.

Acknowledgments

Thank you to the humans who have made it possible for this book to emerge into the world:

- To all of my clients: Thank you for teaching me so much and for letting me share my knowledge.
- To all of the friends who make me want to keep growing and learning: you uphold the best of humanity in your actions and attitudes every day.
  - Ahnna Lake. For being there for all of the epiphanettes.
  - Amber Niehaus. Your stare can move mountains and has helped me fulfill one dream after another.
  - Angela Simpson and Dave Simpson. A) you make me a better human, and B) cupcakes.
  - Barbara Russell. The Rice Krispies treatment was only the beginning.
  - Bob Boyle. You were an excellent boss and teacher. I hope the afterlife is agreeing with you.
  - Danny Hendershot. "Pick up the schmutz and don't be a jackass"—a mantra for work and life.
  - Deborah Garson. For including me in your family and for the moon and tides. *She tried.*
  - Eliza Brown. Fenway Franks are the gateway drug to true friendship.
  - Frank Barrett. For acknowledgments in books and brilliant conversations.
  - Linda Buckley. For coffee, canoes, and wandering through the woods.
  - Nicole Junas Ravlin. You are my Co-princess of Fun—what more is there? It's my pleasure to (be) connect(ed with) you.

- The parents I was lucky to gain along the way, Patty Crandall and Mike Davis.
- My guides and mentors: Alex Forbes, Kate Lingren, and Gale West. Your brilliant gifts of listening and leadership have kept me growing into myself.
- The experts I needed who arrived at the perfect time, Carra Simpson and Jen Louden.
- And to this gifted group of writers: Quincy Gray McMichael, Will Rogers, Kalimah Priforce, Kyra O'Keefe, and Jenny McGibbon. This book would not have happened without you.

For my family in all forms, near and far, past and present: I'm proud to have come from such a long line of characters.

References

Adichie, Chimamanda Ngozi. *We Should All Be Feminists*. United Kingdom: Knopf Doubleday Publishing Group, 2015.

Ajayi, Luvvie. *I'm Judging You: The Do-Better Manual*. United States: Henry Holt and Company, 2016.

Albion, Mark. *True to Yourself: Leading a Values-Based Business*. United Kingdom: Berrett-Koehler Publishers, 2006.

Argyris, C. "Teaching Smart People How to Learn." *Harvard Business Review*, 69(3), 99-109, 1991.

Aristotle. *The Ethics of Aristotle: The Nicomachean Ethics*. (rev. ed.) (J. K. Thomson, trans.). New York: Viking, 1955.

Aristotle. *Aristotle's Art of Rhetoric*. (Robert C. Bartlett, trans.). United States: University of Chicago Press, 2019.

Banaji, Mahzarin R. and Anthony G. Greenwald. *Blindspot: Hidden Biases of Good People*. United Kingdom: Random House Publishing Group, 2016.

Banich, Marie T. *Cognitive Neuroscience and Neuropsychology*. United States: Houghton Mifflin Company, 2004.

Barrett, Frank. *Yes to the Mess: Surprising Leadership Lessons from Jazz*. United States: Harvard Business Review Press, 2012.

Brokaw, Tom. *The Greatest Generation*. United States: Random House Publishing Group, 2004.

Case, John. *Open-Book Management: Coming Business Revolution, The*. United States: HarperCollins, 1996.

Csikszentmihalyi, Mihaly. *The Evolving Self: A Psychology for the Third Millennium*, United Kingdom: HarperCollins, 2009.

Cain, Susan. *Quiet: The Power of Introverts in a World That Can't Stop Talking*. United Kingdom: Crown, 2013.

Covey, Stephen R. *The Seven Habits of Highly Effective People*. United Kingdom: Simon and Schuster, 1989.

Crawford, Matthew B. *Shop Class as Soulcraft: An Inquiry into the Value of Work.* United Kingdom: Penguin Publishing Group, 2010.

Damasio, Antonio. *Descartes' Error: Emotion, Reason, and the Human Brain.* United Kingdom: Penguin Publishing Group, 2005.

Damasio, Antonio R. *The Feeling of what Happens: Body and Emotion in the Making of Consciousness.* United Kingdom: Harcourt Brace, 1999.

Damon, William. *The Moral Advantage: How to Succeed in Business by Doing the Right Thing.* Ukraine: Berrett-Koehler Publishers, 2004.

Damon, William, Howard E. Gardner, and Mihaly Csikszentmihalyi. *Good Work: When Excellence and Ethics Meet.* United States: Basic Books, 2002.

Deming, William Edwards. *The New Economics: For Industry, Government, Education.* United Kingdom: MIT Press, 2000.

Eagly, Alice Hendrickson and Linda Lorene Carli. *Through the Labyrinth: The Truth About How Women Become Leaders.* United States: Harvard Business School Press, 2007.

Egan, Kieran. *Getting It Wrong from the Beginning: Our Progressivist Inheritance from Herbert Spencer, John Dewey, and Jean Piaget.* United Kingdom: Yale University Press, 2002.

Fromm, Erich. *The Art of Listening.* United States: Open Road Media, 2013.

Guenther, Margaret. *Toward Holy Ground: Spiritual Directions for the Second Half of Life.* United States: Cowley Publications, 1995.

Gray, Dave, Sunni Brown, and James Macanufo. *Gamestorming: A Playbook for Innovators, Rulebreakers, and Changemakers.* Japan: O'Reilly Media, 2010.

Hamblett, Charles, and Jane Deverson. *Generation X.* N.p.: London, 1964.

Nikole, Hannah-Jones et al.. *The 1619 Project: A New Origin Story* New York: One World, 2021

Hare, Brian, and Vanessa Woods. *Survival of the Friendliest: Understanding Our Origins and Rediscovering Our Common Humanity.* United States: Random House Publishing Group, 2021.

Immordino-Yang, Mary Helen, and Antonio Damasio. "WE FEEL, THEREFORE WE LEARN." The Jossey-Bass reader on the brain and learning (2007): 183.

Immordino-Yang, Mary Helen. *Emotions, Learning, and the Brain: Embodied Brains, Social Minds and the Art of Learning.* United Kingdom: WW Norton, 2016.

Kellerman, Barbara. *Bad Leadership: What It Is, How It Happens, Why It Matters.* United Kingdom: Harvard Business School Press, 2004.

Lahey, Lisa Laskow, and Robert Kegan. *How the Way We Talk Can Change the Way We Work: Seven Languages for Transformation.* Spain: Wiley, 2012.

Lesser, Elizabeth. *Cassandra Speaks: When Women Are the Storytellers, the Human Story Changes.* United States: HarperCollins, 2020.

Lorde, Audre. "Poetry Is Not a Luxury." *Sister Outsider: Essays and Speeches* (Crossing Press Feminist Series). Berkeley: Clarkson Potter/Ten Speed, 200, pp. 38.

Manton, Elizabeth, Erica Moore, and Rutger Bregman. *Humankind: A Hopeful History.* United States: Little, Brown, 2020.

Moran, Caitlin. *How to be a Woman.* United Kingdom: Ebury Press, 2011.

Noonan, William R. *Discussing the Undiscussable: A Guide to Overcoming Defensive Routines in the Workplace.* Germany: Wiley, 2012.

O'Neill-Blackwell, Jeanine. *Engage: The Trainer's Guide to Learning Styles.* Germany: Wiley, 2012.

O'Neill-Blackwell, Jeanine, and Bernice McCarthy. *Hold On, You Lost Me! Use Learning Styles to Create Training that Sticks.* United States: ASTD Press, 2007.

Ogas, Ogi, and Todd Rose. *Dark Horse: Achieving Success Through the Pursuit of Fulfillment.* United States: HarperCollins, 2018.

Palfrey, John, and Urs Gasser. *Born Digital: Understanding the First Generation of Digital Natives.* Australia: Read How You Want, 2011.

Pennock, Robert T. *An Instinct for Truth: Curiosity and the Moral Character of Science.* United Kingdom: MIT Press, 2019.

Pert, Candace. *Molecules Of Emotion: Why You Feel the Way You Feel.* United Kingdom: Simon & Schuster UK, 2012.

Pinker, Susan. *The Village Effect: How Face-to-Face Contact Can Make Us Healthier and Happier.* United Kingdom: Random House of Canada, 2014.

Post Senning, Daniel, and Lizzie Post. *Emily Post's Etiquette, The Centennial Edition.* United States: Clarkson Potter/Ten Speed, 2022.

Rhode, Deborah, and Barbara Kellerman. *Women & Leadership.* Canada: ExecuGo media, 2007.

Rosenbloom, Stephanie. "Generation Me vs. You Revisited." *The New York Times.* January 17, 2008. https://www.nytimes.com/2008/01/17/fashion/17narcissism.html.

Russell, Penny A., Martin Luther King, Jr., Peter Holloran, Clayborn Carson, and Ralph E. Luker. The Papers of Martin Luther King, Jr., Volume I: Called to Serve, January 1929-June 1951. United Kingdom: University of California Press, 1992, 122-125.

Schur, Mike. *How to Be Perfect: Moral Philosophy from the Creator of THE GOOD PLACE*. United Kingdom: Quercus, 2022.

Seymour, B., and R. Dolan. "Emotion, Decision Making, and the Amygdala." *Neuron*, 58(5), (2008), 662-671

Stabile, Suzanne. The Journey Toward Wholeness: Enneagram Wisdom for Stress, Balance, and Transformation. United Kingdom: InterVarsity Press, 2021.

Stack, Jack, and Bo Burlingham. *The Great Game of Business, Expanded and Updated: The Only Sensible Way to Run a Company*. United States: Crown, 2013.

Steinem, Gloria. *Revolution from Within: A Book of Self-Esteem*. United States: Open Road Media, 2012.

Sutcliffe, Kathleen M., and Karl E. Weick. *Managing the Unexpected: Sustained Performance in a Complex World*. Germany: Wiley, 2015.

Additional Resources

- **Management Models and Organizational Behavior**
- **Emotional and Mental Health**
- **Interesting Things About Cognitive Neuroscience**
- **Good Human Resources Information**

For links to the above topics, the book's worksheets, the illustrated map, and other tools for *Working With Humans*, please go to workingwithhumans.com

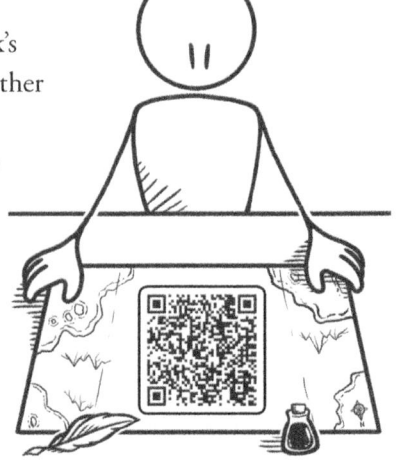

About the Author

Laura Crandall founded her management consulting firm, Slate Communication, in 2009. For over thirty years, she has worked in and consulted with industries that include manufacturing, journalism, hospitality, and academia; fifteen of those years were spent managing teams. Laura's work is dedicated to helping people within organizations discover and develop foundational management and communication skills—the things we assume everyone has, but rarely discuss. She is an instructor in the Career and Academic Resource Center at Harvard Extension School, where she teaches about workplace communication. Laura earned her master's degree from Harvard Graduate School of Education, where she studied cognitive neuroscience and organizational behavior.

A Midwesterner at heart, Laura makes her home among the people of New England. Her favorite date of the year is March 4th—the best day to start new endeavors because it is both a date and an imperative command: March Forth! You can connect with her via her website: *LauraCrandall.com*.

Notes and Reflections

Made in United States
Orlando, FL
03 November 2023